JEREMY HARMER

MERIDIAN

Activity Book 1

Vorwort

Dieses Activity Book ergänzt das Student's Book durch erweiternde und vertiefende Aufgaben. Es bietet zusätzliche Aktivitäten für das Gespräch im Klassenverband und enthält in den Study Sections Aufgaben für die häusliche Nacharbeit - zu inhaltlichen Fragen, zur schriftlichen Arbeit und zur Vertiefung der Grammatik. Weil Ihnen jedoch bei der Erarbeitung der Study Sections nicht immer eine Lehrkraft für Fragen zur Verfügung steht, erhalten Sie zusätzliche Hilfen direkt in den **Study Sections:**

- Alle **Arbeitsanweisungen** erscheinen in deutscher Sprache.

- Die **Language summary** enthält die neuen Wendungen mit deutschen Übersetzungen.

- Die **Grammatik** wird Ihnen in kurzen Anmerkungen mit deutschem Regelwortlaut erklärt.

- In dem Abschnitt **New words** erscheinen alle Wörter, die in den Texten und Hörteilen des Activity Book erstmalig verwendet werden. Bitte beachten Sie, daß die deutschen Übersetzungen sich immer aus dem Zusammenhang ergeben, in dem ein solches Wort steht.

- Der gesamte **Wortschatz des Student's Book** erscheint nach Lektionen geordnet mit deutschen Entsprechungen als Anhang. So können Sie sich zu Hause die Vokabeln gründlich einprägen, die Sie im Kursunterricht kennengelernt haben. Auch hier gilt, daß Sie zunächst nur die Übersetzungen lernen, die für den gerade besprochenen Text von Wichtigkeit sind.

- Alle neuen Wörter werden mit **Lautschrift** angegeben. Die Lautschrift hilft Ihnen, den Klang eines Wortes unabhängig von seiner Schreibung zu erkennen. Eine Übersicht der Lautschriftsymbole mit Schlüsselwörtern steht im Anhang. Bitten Sie Ihren Kursleiter / Ihre Kursleiterin, diese Tabelle mit Ihnen zu besprechen und Ihnen die Lautsymbole zu erklären.

Langenscheidt-Longman
ENGLISH LANGUAGE TEACHING

JEREMY HARMER

MERIDIAN

Activity Book 1

Longman

Longman Group Limited
Longman House, Burnt Mill, Harlow,
Essex CM20 2JE, England

First published 1986

ISBN 0-582-91770-0

Set in 10/12 Univers medium, Linotron 202
by Tradespools Ltd, Frome, Somerset

Printed in Great Britain
by Mackays of Chatham

Illustrated by Tony Kenyon, Charles Front, David Parkins and Jerry Collins
Cover design by Lloyd Northover

German adaptation in Study Sections by Ulrich Rösner

The following symbols are used:

- pairwork
- groups of three
- groupwork
- whole class activity
- teamwork

Interaction

1 :

Look at the pictures. Put the words below in the right speech bubbles.

(In Los Angeles.) (Hello.) (Where do you live?)

(What's your name?) (What do you do?)

2 ∴

In this game **A** shows a sequence of numbers with fingers. **B** says the numbers. **C** writes the numbers down. (*Remember:* **A** does not talk. **C** can't see **A**.)

Listening and acting out 📼

1

Who is talking – **a**, **b** or **c**?

a Anne: housewife   *Tarragona*
b James: teacher   *Oxford*
c Laura: student   *London*

2

Have conversations like the one on the cassette.
Student **A** is a doctor, student **B** a patient.
Student **A** should ask **B** about his/her occupation.
Student **A** fills in the following form about **B**.

NAME:
_____

HOME:
_____

OCCUPATION:
_____

Language summary

Redewendungen

What's your name?
– I'm John.
 What's yours?

Wie heißen Sie?
(Ich heiße) John.
Wie heißen Sie?

Where do you live?
– In London.

Wo wohnen Sie?
In London.

What do you do?
– I'm a doctor.
 What about you?

Was sind Sie von Beruf?
Ich bin Arzt.
Und Sie?

Neue Wörter

my [maɪ]	mein
taxi driver ['tæksɪdraɪvə]	Taxifahrer
thank you ['θæŋkju:]	danke
on holiday [ən'hɒlɪdeɪ]	auf Urlaub

Grammatik

Kurzformen:

I'm = I am   what's = what is

---

1 Berufe

Um welche Berufe handelt es sich? Bringen Sie die Buchstaben in die richtige Reihenfolge.

Beispiel: IXTA REVRID = taxi driver

1 TOOCRD ....

2 SUB REVRID ....

3 TTESUND ....

4 SIOFHEUWE ....

5 MISSESUBANN ....

6 TECRAYRES ....

7 CATEHER ....

---

2 am, is, do

Setzen Sie das richtige Wort ein.

1 What .... your name?   – I..................... Steve.

2 What .... you do?   – I..................... a teacher.

3 Where .... you live?   – In Rome.

4 What .... your name?   – I..................... Lucy.

5 Where .... you live?   – In New York.

3 what, where

Setzen Sie das richtige Wort ein.

1 .... do you live?   – In London.

2 .... do you do?   – I am a student.

3 .... do you live?   – In New York.

4 .... is your name?   – I am Peter.

5 .... do you do?   – I am a businessman.

4 Fragen

Ergänzen Sie den Dialog.

A: ....

B: Hello.

A: ....?

B: I'm Peter Hedley.

A: Oh . . . .?

B: I'm an actor.

A: ....?

B: In London.

5 Lesen und schreiben Sie

Hello! My name is Hugh Rodgers. I live in Edinburgh and I am a taxi driver. What about you? What do you do? Where do you live?

Schreiben Sie einen ähnlichen Text über sich selbst.

....

....

....

....

2 Classwork

Interaction

1:

Read the text and fill in Julio's family tree.

> Hello! My name is Julio. I am married to a lovely lady called Teresa. We have two sons (Vasco and Carlos) and a daughter, Maria. My father, Francisco, is retired and my mother, Rosa, is a dentist. My brother, Rodrigo, is in France now and my sister, Clara, is at home with my parents.

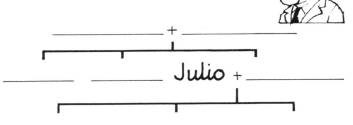

2::

Draw family trees about each other's families.
A tells **B**, **C** and **D** about her family. **B**, **C** and **D** draw the family tree and write in the names of the professions of **A**'s family. The group makes family trees for **B**, **C** and **D** in the same way.

My brother, Peter, is a doctor.

3:

Student **A**: Look at number 1 on page 75. Complete the chart by asking **B** questions.
Student **B**: Look at number 1 on page 81. Complete the chart by asking **A** questions.
Do not look at each other's charts until you have finished.

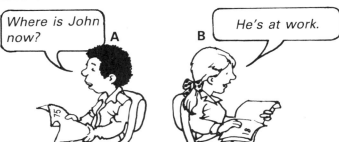

Where is John now?

He's at work.

Listening and acting out 🔊

1

Who is the girl in the picture? (Charlotte or Jane?)

2

Write *Jane, her mother* and *her father* under the correct pictures.

....

3

Have conversations like the one on the cassette.

Ask if someone is there.
Ask where they are.

2 Study section

Language summary

Redewendungen

Is your brother a doctor? – Yes, he is./No, he isn't.	Ist Ihr Bruder Arzt? Ja./Nein.
What does your brother do? – He's a student.	Was ist Ihr Bruder von Beruf? Er ist Student.
Where does he live? – In London.	Wo wohnt er? In London.
Where's Peter? – He's at work.	Wo ist Peter? Er ist zur Arbeit.
Is Fumiko there?	Ist Fumiko da?
please	bitte
OK	in Ordnung
thank you	danke
goodbye	auf Wiedersehen

Neue Wörter

family tree ['fæməli triː]	Stammbaum
married ['mærid]	verheiratet
lovely ['lʌvli]	lieb(enswert)
lady ['leɪdi]	Frau
called [kɔːld]	genannt
we [wiː]	wir
have [hæv]	haben
retired [rɪ'taɪəd]	pensioniert
France [frɑːns]	Frankreich
parents ['peərənts]	Eltern
boyfriend ['bɔɪfrend]	Freund, Verlobter
engineer [ˌendʒɪ'nɪə]	Ingenieur
with me [wɪð'miː]	mit mir

Grammatik

I am	ich bin
you are	du bist/Sie sind
he is	er ist
she is	sie ist
it is	es ist
we are	wir sind
you are	ihr seid/Sie sind
they are	sie sind
I live	ich wohne/lebe
you live	du wohnst/lebst
	Sie wohnen/leben
he lives	er wohnt/lebt
she lives	sie wohnt/lebt
it lives	es wohnt/lebt
we live	wir wohnen/leben
you live	ihr wohnt/lebt
	Sie wohnen/leben
they live	sie wohnen/leben

Fragesätze

What do I do?	Was mache ich?
What do you do?	Was machst du/machen Sie?
What does he do?	Was macht er?
What does she do?	Was macht sie?
What does it do?	Was macht es?
What do we do?	Was machen wir?
What do you do?	Was macht ihr/machen Sie?
What do they do?	Was machen sie?
Where do I live?	Wo wohne ich?
Where do you live?	Wo wohnst du/wohnen Sie?
Where does he live?	Wo wohnt er?
Where does she live?	Wo wohnt sie?
Where does it live?	Wo wohnt es?
Where do we live?	Wo wohnen wir?
Where do you live?	Wo wohnt ihr/wohnen Sie?
Where do they live?	Wo wohnen sie?

Fragesätze ohne *is* brauchen eine Form von *do.*

Ja und nein

Im Englischen gilt es als unhöflich, nur mit *ja* oder *nein* zu antworten. Daher wird das Hilfsverb wiederholt. Wenn kein Hilfsverb vorhanden ist, nimmt man eine Form von *do.*

1 Telefonnummern

Welche Nummer gehört zu welchem Ausdruck?
Füllen Sie das Schema aus.

a 3-3-7-6	**1** two-nine-eight-seven	**a** _11_
b 5-9-2-8	**2** nine-oh-five-six	**b**
c 1-4-9-0	**3** two-four-two-five	**c**
d 3-3-6-7	**4** two-eight-six-five	**d**
e 1-0-9-2	**5** one-four-nine-oh	**e**
f 2-9-8-7	**6** six-two-three-oh	**f**
g 2-8-6-5	**7** five-nine-two-eight	**g**
h 9-0-5-6	**8** one-oh-nine-two	**h**
i 6-2-3-0	**9** three-two-oh-seven	**i**
j 3-2-0-7	**10** three-three-six-seven	**j**
k 2-4-2-5	**11** three-three-seven-six	**k**

2 am, is, are

Setzen Sie die richtige Form ein.

1 I .... a student.

2 My brother .... at home.

3 .... your father at work? – Yes, he ....

4 My sister and brother .... at school.

5 .... you a student? – Yes, I ....

3 do, does

Setzen Sie die richtige Form ein.

1 What .... you do? – I'm a student.

2 What .... your father do? – He's a doctor.

3 Where .... your brother live? – In Sydney.

4 Where .... you live? – In Manchester.

5 Where .... your two sisters live?
– In London.

4 Fragen

Schauen Sie sich das Bild an, und ergänzen Sie den Dialog.

A: .... your brother?

B: Yes, he is.

A: .... a doctor?

B: No, he isn't.

A: ....?

B: He's a dentist.

A: ....?

B: In Oxford.

A: ....?

B: He's at work.

5 Lesen und schreiben Sie

Lesen Sie den Text:

I am Carmen and I am a student. I am at home now. My mother is at work and my brother is at school. My boyfriend, Miguel, is an engineer. He is at home with me now.

Schreiben Sie einen ähnlichen Text über sich selbst.

....

....

....

....

....

....

....

....

Interaction

1

Look at the symbols before playing the game. Listen to the teacher. Put a cross on the correct square when you hear the words. Shout *Bingo!* when all your squares are full.

Symbols:

✚ hospital   🚁 helicopter |◯| restaurant   🏠 house

▓ post office   ⸝ airport   ✎ pencil   ▭ ruler

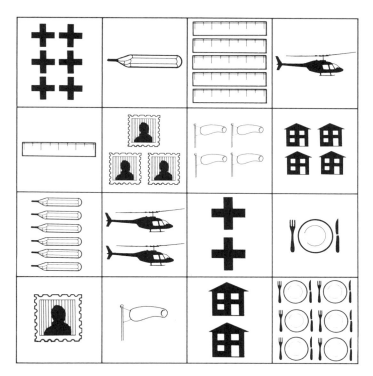

2 :

Student **A**: Look at number 2 on page 75 and complete the task by asking **B** questions.

Student **B**: Look at number 2 on page 81 and complete the task by asking **A** questions.

Do not look at each other's maps until you have finished.

Where does Jim live?

Opposite the Grand Cinema.

Listening and acting out 📼

1

Say whether the statements are true or false.

1 Her father is a doctor.
2 Her mother is a doctor.
3 The man is a policeman.

2

Look at the map. Put a cross for the hospital.

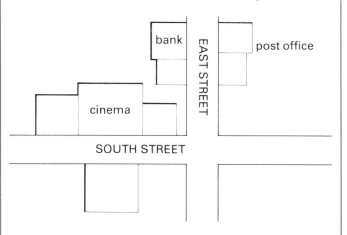

bank   EAST STREET   post office

cinema

SOUTH STREET

3

Student **A** is at home. His father/mother/sister etc. are not at home. Student **B** is doing a survey and arrives at **A**'s home. Student **B** asks about **A**'s father/mother, etc., and their jobs. Where are they now?

3 Study section

Language summary

Redewendungen

Where's the post office?	Wo ist das Postamt?
– It's in Green Street…	Es ist in der Green Street…
opposite the bank	gegenüber der Bank
next to the cinema	neben dem Kino
between the bank and	zwischen der Bank und
the cinema	dem Kino
Excuse me!	Entschuldigen Sie.
– Don't mention it.	Aber gern.
Can I have the glue?	Kann ich den Klebstoff
	haben?
– Of course. Here you are.	Natürlich. Bitte sehr.
Thanks	Danke.

Neue Wörter

airport ['eəpɔːt]	Flughafen
hospital ['hɒspɪtl]	Krankenhaus
box [bɒks]	Schachtel
policeman [pə'liːsmən]	Polizist
central ['sentrəl]	Zentral-/Haupt-
travel agent ['trævleɪdʒənt]	Inhaber oder Angestellter
	eines Reisebüros
travel agency ['trævleɪdʒənsi]	Reisebüro
office ['ɒfɪs]	Büro
too [tuː]	auch

1 Ortsangaben

Um welche Ortsangaben handelt es sich? Bringen Sie die Buchstaben in die richtige Reihenfolge.

Beispiel: NATOTIS = station

1 KANB ....

2 STOPFFIEOC ....

3 TESTURAANR ....

4 NATOTISSUB ....

5 CAIEMN ....

6 ATIRORP ....

2 next to, between, opposite

Schauen Sie sich die Skizze an, und setzen Sie dann das richtige Wort ein.

1 The hospital is .... the cinema.

2 The bank is .... the cinema.

3 The cinema is .... the bank and the restaurant.

4 The post office is .... the theatre.

5 The post office is .... the bus station.

bank	cinema	restaurant		post office	theatre

hospital		bus station

3 am (not), are (not), is (not)

Setzen Sie die richtige Form ein.

1 Are you a businessman? – No, I ....

2 My mother .... a nurse at the Central Hospital.

3 Is your father a teacher? – No, he .... He is a bus driver.

4 Is the cinema opposite the hospital? – Yes, it ....

5 The cinema .... next to the hospital, it is opposite it.

4 Wo ist was?

Schauen Sie sich die Zeichnung an, und ergänzen Sie den Dialog.

A: Can I have the scissors?

B: Yes, of course. **1** .... ?

A: **2** .... the table.

B: Here you are.

A: Thanks. Can I have the glue?

B: Yes. Where **3** .... ?

A: **4** .... the box.

B: Here **5** ....

A: Thanks.

5 Lesen und schreiben Sie

John Richard is a travel agent. He is at work now. His travel agency is in Bridge Street between the post office and the bank. Maggie Shore is a secretary. Her office is in Bridge Street too. It is next to the River Restaurant.

Schreiben Sie einen ähnlichen Text über andere Leute. Berichten Sie, was die Leute von Beruf sind, wo ihr Büro/ihre Wohnung ist und wo sie sich gerade aufhalten.

....

....

....

....

....

....

....

....

....

....

Interaction

1 :::

Team **A**: use this symbol, **O**
Team **B**: use this symbol, **X**
(*Note*: these symbols are called *noughts* and *crosses*.)

1 Choose a square.
2 Make a sentence or a question with the word in the square.
3 Put your team's symbol in the square for a correct response.
4 The first team with a straight line of **O**s or **X**s wins.

can	is	what
where	what	are
is	are	where

how	where	what
is	are	is
can	what	where

2 : :

Fill in the diagram about someone else in the group and their family.

Father
name
age
nationality
home
occupation

Mother
name
age
nationality
home
occupation

....

Brother
name
age
nationality
home
occupation

Sister
name
age
nationality
home
occupation

Listening and acting out 📼

Ray, Patty, Mike and Sam are at a party.

1

Listen to the cassette and put the sentences in the correct order. (Put the numbers 1, 2, or 3 in the boxes.)

RAY: Mike, this is Patty. ☐

RAY: Hello. I'm Ray. ☐

PATTY: Sam, let me introduce Ray and Mike. ☐

2

Listen to the cassette again. Say whether the statements are true or false.

1 Ray is English   T   F

2 Patty is Australian.   T   F

3 Patty lives in Paris.   T   F

4 Patty is a designer.   T   F

5 Patty is twenty-five years old.   T   F

3

You are at a party and you do not know anybody. You can talk about: name
home
occupation
nationality
age

4 Study section

Language summary

Redewendungen

Where's Pedro from?	Wo kommt Pedro her?
– He's from Mexico.	Er ist aus Mexiko.
He's Mexican.	Er ist Mexikaner.
Where are you from?	Wo kommst du her?/Wo kommen Sie her?
– I'm from England.	Ich komme aus England.
I'm English.	Ich bin Engländer (in).
Are you English?	Bist du/sind Sie Engländer (in)?
– Yes, I am./No, I'm not.	Ja./Nein.
How old . . .	Wie alt . . .
is Carmen?	ist Carmen?
are you?	bist du/sind Sie?
– She's/I'm nineteen.	Sie ist/ich bin neunzehn.
I'm Marie and this is Jean Paul.	Ich heiße Marie, und das ist Jean Paul.
– Pleased to meet you.	Angenehm.
– Hi.	Hallo.
That's (= That is) a secret.	Das ist ein Geheimnis.

Neue Wörter

Irish ['aɪərɪʃ]	irisch, Ire/Irin
party ['pɑːti]	Party
designer [dɪ'zaɪnə]	Designer(in)
musician [mjuːˈzɪʃn]	Musiker(in)
dancer ['dɑːnsə]	Tänzer(in)

1 Länder und Völker

Wie nennt man die Bewohner der einzelnen Länder? Tragen Sie sie in die richtige Spalte ein.
Die ersten vier stehen bereits da. Kontrollieren Sie Ihre Lösungen dann anhand der Angaben auf Seite 88.

Mexico
England
Japan
France
Portugal
Switzerland
Puerto Rico
Spain
Germany
America
Australia
China
Brazil
Saudi Arabia
Peru
Hungary
Denmark
Sweden
Turkey
Italy
Greece
Argentina
Holland
Belgium
Yugoslavia
Ireland

-an	-ish	-ese	irregular
Mexican	English	Japanese	French

2 Zur Wiederholung

Welche Frage paßt zu welcher Antwort? Füllen Sie das Schema aus.

1 What's your name?	**a** No, she is not.	**1** _b_
2 Where do you live?	**b** Michael.	**2** ....
3 What do you do?	**c** In Green Street next to the church.	**3** ....
4 Where is your house?	**d** I am a musician.	**4** ....
5 What does your sister do?	**e** She is a dancer.	**5** ....
6 Is she at home now?	**f** At work.	**6** ....
7 Where is she?	**g** In Manchester.	**7** ....

3 Wo kommen Sie her?

Füllen Sie die Lücken aus (es fehlt jeweils nur *ein* Wort).

1 Is he from America? – No, he is .... He is Australian.

2 .... is Kate from? – She is from Lisbon. She is Portuguese.

3 Gerry and Bernadette are not from England. They .... Irish.

4 Marie is from Switzerland. She is ....

5 Is Raul .... Colombia? – No he is not. He is Bolivian.

4 where, what, how old

Setzen Sie das richtige Wort ein.

1 .... is Monica from? – She is English.

2 .... does she live? – In Singapore.

3 .... does she do? – She is a student.

4 .... is she? – Twenty.

5 .... is her house? – Opposite the First National Bank.

5 Dialog

Sie treffen Pete und Mary auf einer Party. Was antworten Sie Pete?

PETE: Hello.

YOU: **1** ....

PETE: I'm Pete and this is Mary.

YOU: **2** ....

PETE: What's your name?

YOU: **3** ....

PETE: And where are you from?

YOU: **4** ....

PETE: Really! What do you do?

YOU: **5** ....

PETE: We're teachers. And where do you live?

YOU: **6** ....

5 Classwork

Interaction

1 :

Look at the pictures. Put the words below in the right speech bubbles.

Hello.   Hi.

At the disco.

At the disco?
Who with?

What
does he
do?

(Kostas.) (Where's he from?)

(He's a pilot.) (Greece.)

Where were you
yesterday evening?

2 :

Choose someone in the class and complete this chart about them.

NAME: .... AGE: ....

HOME: ....

OCCUPATION: ....

NATIONALITY: ....

MOVEMENTS:

1 ten o'clock yesterday morning

....

2 three o'clock yesterday afternoon

....

3 five o'clock yesterday afternoon

....

4 nine o'clock yesterday evening

....

Listening and acting out 📼

1

Listen to the cassette and answer the questions.

1 The inspector thinks:
   a Charlie's a policeman.
   b Charlie's a thief.
   c Charlie's a doctor.

2 Where was Charlie:
   a at nine o'clock?
   b at ten o'clock?

3 Who was Charlie with at ten o'clock?

2

Look. This was the bank at 10 o'clock last night.

Student **A** is a policeman. Ask the others about last night. Were they the thieves?

Where were you
at ten o'clock?

5 Study section

Language summary

Redewendungen

Were you at home yesterday evening?
– Yes, I was./No, I wasn't (= was not).

Warst du/Waren Sie gestern abend zu Hause? Ja./Nein.

Where were you on Monday afternoon?
– I was at the bank.

Wo warst du/waren Sie Montag nachmittag? Ich war in der Bank.

What's (= What is) the time?
– It's ten o'clock.

Wie spät ist es? Es ist zehn Uhr.

Fumiko speaking.
– I forgot. I'm sorry.

Hier ist Fumiko. Entschuldigung, das hatte ich vergessen.

Neue Wörter

think [θɪŋk] — denken
thief [θiːf] — Dieb
girlfriend ['gɜːlfrend] — Freundin
until [ən'tɪl] — bis
Canadian [kə'neɪdjən] — kanadisch, Kanadier(in)
last [lɑːst] — der/die/das letzte/vergangene
night [naɪt] — Abend/Nacht

Grammatik

Im Englischen steht die Ortsangabe immer vor der Zeitangabe: Were you *at home yesterday afternoon*?

Die *Vergangenheitsformen* (past tense) von *be* (= sein).

I was	ich war
you were	du warst/Sie waren
she was	sie war
he was	er war
it was	es war
we were	wir waren
you were	ihr wart/Sie waren
they were	sie waren

1 Ortsangaben

Suchen Sie die anderen fünf Ortsangaben, und kreisen Sie sie ein.

C	A	D	I	S	C	O	B	C	D	S	E
F	D	G	H	I	F	J	K	M	M	O	N
O	P	E	Q	R	G	S	T	N	V	P	W
S	U	P	E	R	M	A	R	K	E	T	Q
X	A	Z	K	Y	H	C	I	N	E	M	A
E	F	N	G	K	J	H	H	L	N	Q	K
M	A	Z	S	T	A	T	I	O	N	R	R
B	A	E	T	I	L	K	O	G	T	M	U
T	X	P	W	L	N	N	Z	V	M	E	Q
H	O	S	P	I	T	A	L	O	Y	J	L

14

2 Zeitangaben

Schreiben Sie die Uhrzeit auf wie in Beispiel 1.

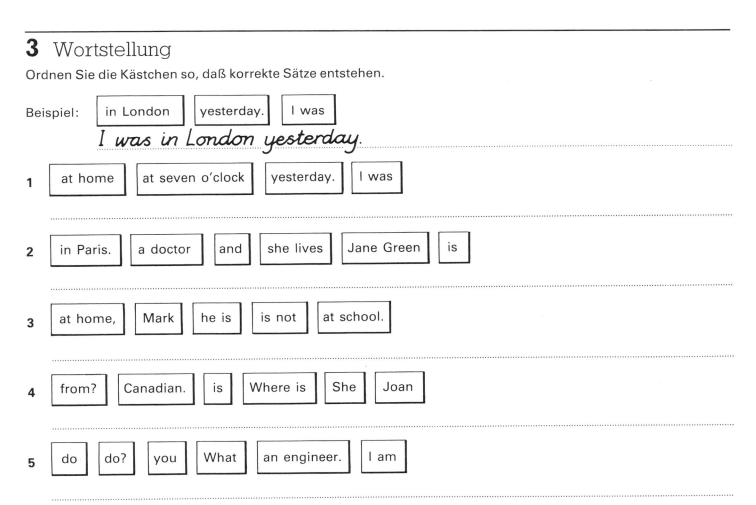

1 *It is 3 o'clock.* ....

2 ....

3 ....

4 ....

5 ....

6 ....

7 ....

8 ....

9 ....

10 ....

3 Wortstellung

Ordnen Sie die Kästchen so, daß korrekte Sätze entstehen.

Beispiel: | in London | yesterday. | I was |

I was in London yesterday. ....

1 | at home | at seven o'clock | yesterday. | I was |

....

2 | in Paris. | a doctor | and | she lives | Jane Green | is |

....

3 | at home, | Mark | he is | is not | at school. |

....

4 | from? | Canadian. | is | Where is | She | Joan |

....

5 | do | do? | you | What | an engineer. | I am |

....

4 was, were

Setzen Sie *was* oder *were* ein (mit oder ohne *not*).

1 .... you at the cinema yesterday evening? – No, I ....

2 Yesterday morning Mr Jones .... at the bank.

3 Yesterday evening Philip and Susan .... at the disco.

4 At seven o'clock Mr and Mrs Scofield .... at the theatre, they were at the cinema.

5 Yesterday afternoon I .... at home with my mother.

5 Lesen und schreiben Sie

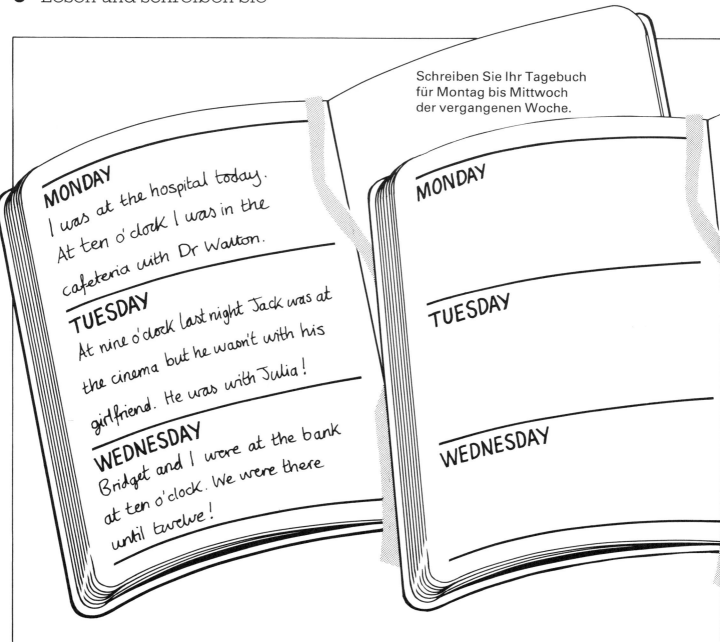

Schreiben Sie Ihr Tagebuch
für Montag bis Mittwoch
der vergangenen Woche.

MONDAY
I was at the hospital today.
At ten o'clock I was in the
cafeteria with Dr Walton.

TUESDAY
At nine o'clock last night Jack was at
the cinema but he wasn't with his
girlfriend. He was with Julia!

WEDNESDAY
Bridget and I were at the bank
at ten o'clock. We were there
until twelve!

MONDAY

TUESDAY

WEDNESDAY

6 Classwork

Interaction

1 :

Decide which clothes are Jane's and which are Kate's.
Ask *Whose skirt is this?* etc.

Jane   Kate

2 :·:

Look at the symbols before you play the game.
Listen to the teacher. Put a cross on the correct square
when you hear the words. Shout *Bingo!* when all the
squares are full.

Symbols: ✂ scissors 🔲 lighter ▭ ruler 👉 this
        pen sellotape that

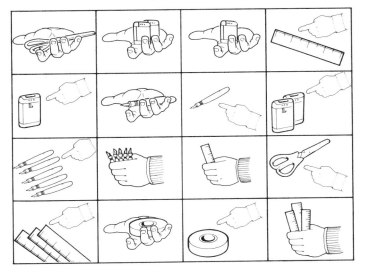

Listening and acting out 📼

1

Listen to the cassette and answer the questions.

1 Where are George and Judith?
2 Whose hat is it?
3 Whose coat is it?
4 Whose party is it?

2

Choose the correct answers.

1 What time is it?
a ten o'clock
b eleven o'clock
c twelve o'clock

2 Where were the gloves?

3

At the end of a party you go home.
  Talk about the time.
  Get your hats, coats and gloves.
  Say goodbye and thank you.

Language summary

Redewendungen

Whose sweater is this/ that?	Wem gehört dieser Pullover/der Pullover dort? Wessen . . . ist dies/das?
– It's (= it is) John's.	Er gehört John. Es ist Johns.
Whose shoes are these/ those? – They are mine/yours/ his/hers.	Wessen Schuhe sind das hier/dort? Das sind meine/deine (Ihre)/seine/ihre.
Is this yours? Can I borrow it/them? . . . I think.	Gehört das dir (Ihnen)? Kann ich es/sie leihen? . . . glaube ich.

Neue Wörter

hat [hæt]	Hut
coat [kəʊt]	Mantel
dress [dres]	Kleid
photograph ['fəʊtəgrɑːf]	Foto
police station [pə'liːs'steɪʃn]	Polizeiwache
(bus) depot [('bʌs) 'depəʊ]	(Bus-) Depot
waiter ['weɪtə]	Kellner

Grammatik

Mit *this* bezeichnet man einen Gegenstand, der sich in Reichweite befindet. Mit *that* bezeichnet man einen Gegenstand, der weiter entfernt ist.

Die Mehrzahl von *this* heißt *these*.
Die Mehrzahl von *that* heißt *those*.

---

1 Kleidungsstücke

Setzen Sie Buchstaben so ein, daß die Namen von Kleidungsstücken entstehen. Ziehen Sie dann einen Kreis um *his* oder *hers,* je nachdem ob es sich um ein Kleidungsstück für einen Mann oder eine Frau handelt.

Beispiel: T _ I _ E _ (his)/hers

1 G — — S — — —   his/hers   **5** T — — — S — — —   his/hers

2 D — E — —   his/hers   **6** S — — — T — —   his/hers

3 B — — — S   his/hers   **7** J — — — E —   his/hers

4 S — O — —   his/hers   **8** S — — R —   his/hers

---

2 this, that, these, those

Setzen Sie die richtige Form ein.

1  .... are scissors.

3 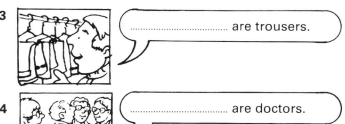 .... are trousers.

2 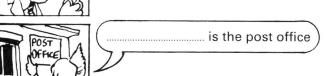 .... is the post office

4 .... are doctors.

5 .... is my tie.

6 .... is my home.

7 .... is my bank.

8 .... are pens.

---

3 mine, his, hers, ours, theirs und whose

Setzen Sie das richtige Wort ein.

Beispiel: ___Whose___ pen is this? – It is ___his.___

1 .... house is that? – It is ....

2 Whose gloves .... these? – They are ....

3 .... pencil .... this? – It is ....

4 .... matches .... these? – They are ....

5 Whose lighter is this? ....

---

4 Allgemeine Wiederholung

Wählen Sie die richtige Form aus (a oder b).

Beispiel: I $\begin{smallmatrix} \mathbf{a} \text{ were} \\ \mathbf{b} \text{ was} \end{smallmatrix}$ in London. ___b___

1 John $\begin{smallmatrix} \mathbf{a} \text{ lives} \\ \mathbf{b} \text{ live} \end{smallmatrix}$ in London. ....

2 Mark is not $\begin{smallmatrix} \mathbf{a} \text{ in} \\ \mathbf{b} \text{ at} \end{smallmatrix}$ home, he is at school. ....

3 Where $\begin{smallmatrix} \mathbf{a} \text{ John's house is?} \\ \mathbf{b} \text{ is John's house?} \end{smallmatrix}$ ....

4 What $\begin{smallmatrix} \mathbf{a} \text{ do} \\ \mathbf{b} \text{ does} \end{smallmatrix}$ you do? ....

5 John is from $\begin{smallmatrix} \mathbf{a} \text{ English;} \\ \mathbf{b} \text{ England;} \end{smallmatrix}$ Mary is from France. ....

5 Lesen und schreiben Sie

This is my sister. Her name is Mary. She is a bus driver and she lives in London. That is her house in the photograph. Mary's bus depot is in Kennington Road, but she lives in William Road, next to the police station. Mary's husband is Italian and he is a waiter. His name is Nino. Mary is with Nino in this photograph.

Kleben Sie hier das Foto eines Familienmitgliedes ein, und schreiben Sie über die abgebildete Person einen ähnlichen Text wie oben.

7 Classwork

Interaction

1:

a In pairs put the sentences in the correct order to make a dialogue. Number the sentences. The first sentence is already numbered for you.

> **1** Good morning. Can I help you?

> When do you want your appointment?

> Goodbye.

> Ten o'clock? Yes. Thank you very much.

> Good morning. I want an appointment with Doctor Fowler.

> Yes, that's OK. Can you come at ten o'clock?

> On Thursday the 9th, if that's all right.

2:

a Find out the meaning of these words. (Ask your teacher or use a dictionary.)

sitting room, dining room, bathroom, kitchen, studio, bedroom, guest room.

b Student **A**: Look at number 3 on page 76. Put the names in the correct rooms by asking **B**.
Student **B**: Look at number 3 on page 82. Put the names in the correct rooms by asking **A**.
Do not look at each other's plans until you have finished.

> *Where was Kate at half past eight?*

> *Where were Tony and Mark at quarter to eleven?*

Listening and acting out 📼

1

Listen to the cassette and answer the questions.

1 Where does Miss Shore want to go?
2 Does she want first class or tourist class?
3 Who is the extra seat for?

2

Listen to the cassette again and complete the chart.

| NAME: .... |
| ADDRESS: .... |
| .... |

FLIGHT TO	DATE
1	
2	
3	
4	

Student **A** is a travel agent
Student **B** rings up to book a flight

Talk about:
   Where? (Madrid, New York, etc.)
   When? (27th February, 4th March, etc.)
   What class? (first class/tourist class)

7 Study section

Language summary

1 Datumsangaben

Ordnen Sie die Wörter den Datumsangaben zu.

a	1/1	1	the fifth of April	a	7	
b	5/4	2	the seventeenth of March	b		
c	4/7	3	the twenty-seventh of April	c		
d	17/3	4	the thirty-first of August	d		
e	22/10	5	the eleventh of February	e		
f	31/8	6	the fourth of July	f		
g	11/2	7	the first of January	g		
h	27/4	8	the twenty-second of October	h		

2 Zeitangaben

Schreiben Sie neben jede Uhr die entsprechende Uhrzeit.

1   *It is half past nine.*

2

3

4

5

6

3 Großschreibung

Ziehen Sie einen Kreis um die Wörter, die groß
geschrieben werden.

Beispiel: (june) businessman (moscow) (We write *June* and *Moscow*.)

john   teacher   chemist's   holland   beach   gloves   bank   mother

son   spanish   jacket   trousers   home   jane   anna   pilot   ankara

paris   january   agatha christie   sailor   supermarket

4 what, when, where, whose

Setzen Sie die richtige Form ein.

1 .... do you do? – I am a student.

2 .... were you yesterday afternoon? – At the restaurant.

3 .... is your house? – In Newmarket Road opposite the school.

4 .... is your birthday? – 24th January.

5 .... do you live? – In Cambridge.

6 .... house is this? – It is mine.

7 .... are you from? – I am Turkish.

8 .... is your sister? – She is at work.

5 Lesen und schreiben Sie

Julio Branco is a Portuguese diplomat from Lisbon.
Julio is fifty-six years old and his birthday is
on 10th August. Julio was in Brazil from
1975–1982. Now he lives in Vila Franca with his
wife, Teresa, and their three children.

Schreiben Sie einen ähnlichen Text über Tom King.

Name: Tom King
Nationality: Australian (Sydney)
Parents' home: Sydney
Age: 36
Birthday: 15/9
Visit: England, 1980–1984
Present home: Cedar Road, Sydney
Marital status: single

....

....

....

....

....

....

....

....

Schreiben Sie jetzt einen Text über eine
Person aus Ihrem eigenen Land.

....

Interaction

1:

Complete this paragraph with information about another student.

(Name) _____ is _____
years old. She/he is from _____
and she/he lives in _____.
Her/his birthday is on _____.
When she/he was ten years old her/his favourite
food was _____ and her/his
favourite song was _____.
_____ likes music, and she/he likes
_____ best, but she/he does
not like _____.

2 ::

a Fill in the subject column in the survey form with the names of famous sportsmen, singers, actors, etc.

b Ask people if they like the personalities in your survey. Record their answers with a tick (√) for yes, a cross (×) for no, and a question mark (?) 'don't know'.

Subject	yes	no	don't know

Listening and acting out 📼

1

Listen to the cassette and answer the questions.

1 What does Bart Scott do?
2 Where is Bart Scott from?
3 Where does he live now?

2

Listen to the cassette again and say whether the statements are true or false.

1 Bart does not like India.   T F
2 Bart likes curry.   T F
3 Bart likes New York best.   T F
4 Bart likes his own music best.   T F

3

Student **A** is a famous 'celebrity', student **B** is an interviewer on a television programme. **B** asks **A** about his home, nationality, likes and dislikes, etc.

Language summary

Redewendungen

Do you like steak?	Magst du/Mögen Sie Steak?
– Yes, I do./No, I don't (= do not).	Ja./Nein.
– I don't know, I've (= I have) never tried it.	Ich weiß nicht, das habe ich noch nie probiert.
What's spaghetti bolognese?	Was ist Spaghetti Bolognese?
– It's an Italian dish with pasta and minced meat.	Das ist ein italienisches Gericht mit Nudeln und Hackfleisch.
What's (= What is) your favourite sport?	Was ist dein/Ihr Lieblingssport?
– I like running best.	– Ich mag Laufen am liebsten.
I like running too.	Ich mag Laufen auch.
– I don't.	Ich nicht.

Neue Wörter

rice [raɪs]	Reis
chicken ['tʃɪkɪn]	Hähnchen
seafood ['siːfuːd]	Meeresfrüchte
rowing ['rəʊɪŋ]	Rudern
song [sɒŋ]	Lied
famous ['feɪməs]	berühmt
music ['mjuːzɪk]	Musik
subject [səb'dʒekt]	Subjekt/Satzgegenstand
India ['ɪndɪə]	Indien
steward ['stjʊəd]	Steward
dancing [dɑːnsɪŋ]	Tanzen
films [fɪlmz]	Filme
likes [laɪks]	mag
dislikes [dɪs'laɪks]	mag nicht
how boring [ˌhaʊ'bɔːrɪŋ]	wie langweilig
both [bəʊθ]	beide
country ['kʌntri]	Land
fantastic [fæn'tæstɪk]	phantastisch

Grammatik

Fragen

I ich	like mag	_____	**do**	**I**	like? mag ich?		**it** es	**likes** mag	_____	**does it** mag	**like?** es?
you du Sie	like magst mögen	_____	**do**	**you** magst mögen	like? du? Sie?		**we** wir	**like** mögen	_____	**do we** mögen	**like?** wir?
he er	likes mag	_____	**does he** mag		**like?** er?		**you** ihr Sie	**like** mögt mögen	_____	**do you** mögt mögen	**like?** ihr? Sie?
she sie	likes mag	_____	**does she** mag		**like?** sie?		**they** sie	**like** mögen	_____	**do they** mögen	**like?** sie?

Fragen werden mit einer Form von *do* gebildet. Diese Form erscheint nicht in der Übersetzung.

Großschreibung

Nach einem Punkt wird immer groß geschrieben.

---

1 Sport

Schreiben Sie die Sportarten unter die Bilder.

1

rowing

2

3

4

5

6

7

8

2 do, does

Setzen Sie die richtige Form ein.

1 Where .... you live? – in Paris.

2 What .... John do? – He's a teacher.

3 Where .... your mother and father live? – In London.

4 .... Peter like raw fish? – No, he does not.

5 My friends John and Mary .... not like paella.

6 .... you like paella? – Yes, I love it.

3 Großschreibung

Ziehen Sie Kreise um die Wörter, die mit einem Großbuchstaben beginnen müssen.

Beispiel: (tom) is an actor. (he) lives in (sydney). (We write *Tom*,

Sydney and *He*.) *He* has a capital letter here because
it is the first word in the sentence.

christopher williams is a steward for an airline. he is married to sharon.
she is a pilot and they live in uxbridge.

last night christopher and sharon were at the disco. sharon likes dancing,
but christopher does not. he likes films best.

4 Gespräch übers Essen

Ergänzen Sie den Dialog.

1 Have some houmous.

3 Do you like moussaka?

5 It's a (Greek, aubergines, cheese, minced meat)

....

.... Do you want some?

7 What's your favourite food, then?

9 Oh, how boring! Don't you like any Greek food?

11 Well then! Now's the time! Waiter!

2 No thank you! I .... like it!

4 What is it?

6 No, thank you.

8 Well, I think I like shepherd's pie ....

10 I don't know. I've .... tried it.

5 Lesen und schreiben Sie

Carol's Cooking Page

In February and March last year I was on holiday. From 24th February to 6th March, I was in France, and from 6th March to 18th March, I was in Spain.

The food in both countries was fantastic, but I like paella best! It is a Spanish dish with rice, chicken and seafood. I had paella when I was in Valencia.

Carol in Spain

Carol war in Deutschland/Österreich/der Schweiz. Schreiben Sie Carols "Kochseite" nach diesem Besuch.

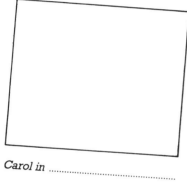

Carol's Cooking Page

Carol in ....

9 Classwork

Interaction

1

Ask other students questions to complete the chart.

> Find someone who:
>
> **a** plays a musical instrument ....
>
> **b** was at a restaurant last night ....
>
> **c** reads a newspaper after breakfast ....
>
> **d** likes rock music ....
>
> **e** goes jogging ....

2

Student **A**: Look at number 4 on page 76. Complete the chart by asking **B** and **C**.
Student **B**: Look at number 4 on page 82. Complete the chart by asking **A** and **C**.
Student **C**: Look at number 4 on page 87. Complete the chart by asking **A** and **B**.

Do not look at each other's charts until you have finished.

> What time does flight 389 leave?

> Which is the gate for the flight to Paris?

> Where does flight 951 go?

> What time does flight 006 arrive?

3

Complete the blanks with information from the flight timetable.

1 A: Which is the gate for the flight to Mexico City?

B: .... It leaves at ....

A: Help! That's in five minutes!

2 A: Stewardess! What number is this flight?

B: 027.

A: Where ....?

B: ....

A: Oh no! I want flight .... to Paris.

Listening and acting out 📼

1

Listen to the cassette and fill in the chart.

> NAME: *Angela Stansgate*
>
> SYMPTOMS:
> *Where is the pain?*   stomach ☐
>
> chest ☐
>
> head ☐
>
> legs ☐
>
> HABITS: **yes**   **no**
> *Does the patient*
> smoke? ☐ ☐
>
> take exercise? ☐ ☐

2

Listen to the cassette again and write down the doctor's recommendations.

> DOCTOR'S RECOMMENDATIONS
>
> 1 _____
>
> 2 _____
>
> 3 _____

3

Have similar conversations. Student **A** is the doctor, student **B** is the patient. The doctor should ask the patient about the pain and his/her habits. The doctor should make recommendations.

Language summary

Redewendungen

What time do you have breakfast? – At half past seven.	Wann frühstückst du/frühstücken Sie? Um halb acht.
How do you go to work? – By car./On foot.	Wie kommst du/kommen Sie zur Arbeit? Mit dem Auto./Zu Fuß.
What do you do in the evening? – I usually listen to music.	Was machst du/machen Sie am Abend/abends? Für gewöhnlich höre ich Musik.
How much is a return ticket to King's Lynn?	Was kostet eine Rückfahrkarte nach King's Lynn?
Which is the platform for King's Lynn?	Von welchem Bahnsteig fährt der Zug nach King's Lynn?
That's in four minutes.	Das ist in vier Minuten.

Neue Wörter

drive [draɪv]	fahren
musical instrument ['mju:zikl 'instrəmənt]	Musikinstrument
smoke [sməʊk]	rauchen
take exercise [ˌteɪk'eksəsaɪz]	Sport treiben
cards [kɑːdz]	Karten
gate [geɪt]	Eingang
stewardess [ˌstjʊə'des]	Stewardess
newspaper ['nju:sˌpeɪpə]	Zeitung
stomach ['stʌmək]	Magen
chest [tʃest]	Brust (kasten)
head [hed]	Kopf
legs [legz]	Beine
pain [peɪn]	Schmerz
bath [baːθ]	Bad
the movies [ðə'muːviːz]	Kino
every ['evrɪ]	jeder
ambulance ['æmbjʊləns]	Krankenwagen
garage ['gærɑːʒ]	Werkstatt
private ['praɪvət]	privat
language ['læŋgwɪdʒ]	Sprache
class [klɑːs]	Klasse
everyday ['evrɪdeɪ]	jeden Tag
start [stɑːt]	anfangen
optional ['ɒpʃnl]	zusätzlich
principal ['prɪnsəpl]	Schulleiter
United States of America [juːˈnaɪtɪd 'steɪts əv əˈmerɪkə]	Vereinigte Staaten von Amerika
previous ['priːvɪəs]	früher
businesswoman ['bɪznɪswʊmən]	Geschäftsfrau

Grammatik

I	get up		ich stehe auf	
you	get up		du stehst auf/ Sie stehen auf	
he	gets up		er steht auf	
she	gets up		sie steht auf	
it	gets up		es steht auf	
we	get up		wir stehen auf	
you	get up		ihr steht auf/ Sie stehen auf	
they	get up		sie stehen auf	

What time do	I	get up?	Wann stehe ich auf?
What time do	you	get up?	Wann stehst du auf?/ Wann stehen Sie auf?
What time does	he	get up?	Wann steht er auf?
What time does	she	get up?	Wann steht sie auf?
What time does	it	get up?	Wann steht es auf?
What time do	we	get up?	Wann stehen wir auf?
What time do	you	get up?	Wann steht ihr auf?/ Wann stehen Sie auf?
What time do	they	get up?	Wann stehen sie auf?

In Fragen mit *do* verliert das Verb das **s** in der dritten Person Einzahl. Dafür wird an das *do* die Endung **es** angehängt.

1 Aktivitäten für den Alltag und die Freizeit

Verbinden Sie die folgenden Verben und Ausdrücke.

1 read	a	at 6 o'clock	1	*h*
2 watch	b	cards	2	
3 go to	c	music	3	
4 listen to	d	home	4	
5 play	e	a bath	5	
6 arrive	f	swimming	6	
7 get up	g	the movies	7	
8 go	h	a newspaper	8	
9 have	i	by bus	9	
10 travel	j	television	10	

2 Wortstellung

Ordnen Sie die Kästchen so, daß korrekte Sätze
entstehen.

Beispiel:

| in Hong Kong | | yesterday. | | I was |

I was in Hong Kong yesterday.

1 | is | | the hotel | | The Dominion Theatre | | next to | | in Granton Road. |

....

2 | is | | Peter's | | July. | | 21st | | birthday | | on |

....

3 | every morning. | | gets up | | Mary | | at five o'clock |

....

4 | with | | a Spanish dish | | is | | chicken and seafood. | | Paella |

....

5 | on Sundays. | | John | | plays tennis | | usually |

....

3 Verb-Endungen im Präsens

Schreiben Sie die korrekten Formen für die Verben in Klammern in die Lücken.

Beispiel: Peter usually (go) ......*goes*...... jogging in the mornings.

1 Peter is an ambulance driver. He (get) .... up at six o'clock.

2 Peter's two sisters, Mary and Emma, (leave) .... home at
half past seven.

3 Mary and Emma (get) .... to school at quarter to nine.

4 Peter (have) .... lunch at one o'clock.

5 Emma and Mary (have) .... lunch at half past one.

6 Peter (read) .... a newspaper in the evenings.

7 Mary and Emma (go) .... to bed at eleven o'clock.

4 Verstehen und wiederholen

Lesen Sie den Text, und setzen Sie in jede
Lücke nur ein Wort.

Peter is twenty-three years[1] .... and he lives in Birmingham with
[2] .... mother and father.

Every day Peter gets up [3] .... six o'clock and he goes jogging.

Then he has [4] .... and drives to work. [5] ....

gets to the hospital at eight o'clock.

Yesterday Peter's car [6] .... in the garage.

Peter was not at work at eight o'clock, he was on a bus!

[7] .... favourite sport is football but he [8] ....

skiing too. He usually plays tennis at weekends.

5 Lesen und schreiben Sie

Schreiben Sie einen ähnlichen Text über die Mersey
Music School.

Name: Mersey Music School

Students: from England, Canada and the United
States of America.

Daily activities: Classes 8.30–12.30 Lunch 12.45
Drama classes in the afternoon
Evening: read newspapers, play darts/chess

Principal: Angela Naseby, music teacher

Previous job: Businesswoman

Schreiben Sie in gleicher Weise über eine Schule, die
Sie kennen.

The Mill Language School

Until 1932 The Mill was a private hospital but
now it is a language school for students from Italy to Indonesia, from Kuwait to Brazil. Every
day students get to the school at quarter to nine.
Classes start at nine o'clock and lunch is at one.
In the afternoon students go to 'optional'
classes. In the evening they eat at the school
restaurant or watch television in the student TV
room.

The principal of the school is Roger Arnold.
Roger was a singer but now he teaches English.

....

....

....

....

....

....

....

....

....

....

....

10 Classwork

Interaction

1 :::

Read these instructions:

1 Write a different word in each space below.
2 Divide into two teams.
3 A member from team **A** chooses a number from 1 – 16.
4 A member of team **B** says his/her word for that number.
5 The member of team **A** uses that word in a sentence or question. He or she gets a point if the sentence or question is correct.

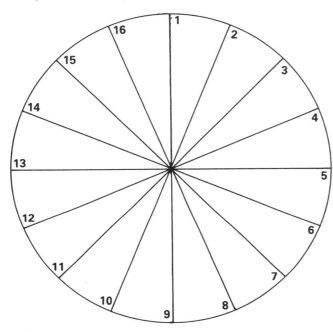

2 :

Student **A**: Look at number 5 on page 77. Find the similarities between your picture and **B**'s by asking **B**.
Student **B**: Look at number 5 on page 83. Find the similarities between your picture and **A**'s by asking **A**.
Do not look at each other's pictures until you have finished.

Is he tall? Is his hair black? How old is he?

Listening and acting out 🔲

SIMON SMOTHER

1

Match George Hayes, Fenella Orchard, Stella Richards and Albert Winterton with their ideal husband or wife.

a a short man with glasses and a beard	**b** a tall thin woman with blue eyes and blond hair
c a tall thin man with grey hair and blue eyes	**d** a short woman with brown eyes and a happy face

2

Have similar conversations. Student **A** works at *Find Your Partner* and student **B** wants a husband/wife. Student **A** asks **B** about the 'ideal' husband/wife.

Ask: short/tall?
       how old?
       colour of eyes?

Language summary

Redewendungen

What colour is Jane's hair?
– It's grey.

Welche Farbe hat Janes Haar?
Es ist grau.

What colour are Jane's eyes?
– They're brown.

Welche Farbe haben Janes Augen?
Sie sind braun.

What does Peter look like?
– He's a fat man with brown hair.

Wie sieht Peter aus?
Er ist dick und hat braune Haare.

Can I help you?

Kann ich dir/Ihnen helfen?

One of ...
A pair of ...
... those sweaters.
... those shoes.

Einer von ...
Ein Paar von ...
... diesen Pullovern da.
... diesen Schuhen da.

Which colour?
What size?

Welche Farbe?
Welche Größe?

Neue Wörter

pink [pɪŋk]	rosa
intelligent [ɪn'telɪdʒənt]	intelligent
stupid ['stuːpɪd]	dumm
big [bɪg]	groß
strong [strɒŋ]	stark
weak [wiːk]	schwach
pretty ['prɪti]	hübsch
handsome ['hæntsəm]	gutaussehend
ugly ['ʌgli]	häßlich
kind [kaɪnd]	freundlich
unkind [ʌn'kaɪnd]	unfreundlich
sad [sæd]	traurig
beard [bɪəd]	Bart
find [faɪnd]	finden
partner ['pɑːtnə]	Partner
dinner ['dɪnə]	(Abend-)Essen
visit ['vɪzɪt]	besuchen
type [taɪp]	maschineschreiben
letters ['letəz]	Briefe
drawer ['drɔː]	Schublade

1 Beschreibende Adjektive

Schreiben Sie aus der folgenden Liste die Gegensatz-Paare heraus.
Sie dürfen ein Wörterbuch benutzen.

tall
intelligent
thin
stupid
small
new
old
fat
kind
old
weak
big
young
pretty
ugly
unkind
happy
handsome
ugly
sad
strong
short

tall, short

2 is/are, was/were

Setzen Sie die richtige Form ein.

1 What colour .... John's tie? – It's blue.

2 Mary and Emma .... young girls.

3 Emma's eyes .... green.

4 Mary's hair .... brown.

5 Mrs Smith's hair .... black, but now it .... white.

6 Mary and Emma .... at the cinema yesterday evening.

7 What colour .... John's trousers? – They .... brown.

3 Beschreibungen

Beschreiben Sie die Personen auf den Bildern jeweils mit einem vollständigen Satz.

brown hair blue eyes	pink hair brown eyes	grey hair green eyes	blond hair blue eyes	white hair brown eyes
1	2	3	4	5

1 ....

2 ....

3 ....

4 ....

5 ....

4 Zur Wiederholung

Wählen Sie die richtige Möglichkeit aus (*a* oder *b*).

Beispiel: **a** were / **b** was in London. ...... *b*

1 Do you like octopus? Yes I **a** do. / **b** like. ....

2 Mary is **a** young girl. / **b** a young girl. ....

3 They **a** has / **b** have dinner at eight o'clock.

4 James is a young man with brown **a** hair. / **b** hairs.

5 **a** This / **b** These are my books. ....

5 Großschreibung und Punkte

Schreiben Sie den folgenden Text ab. Setzen Sie dabei Punkte, wo
es nötig ist, und denken Sie an die Großschreibung nach einem Punkt.

Beispiel: john is a businessman he lives in London

John is a businessman. He lives in London.

alistair is thirty-two years old he is a doctor and he lives in london alistair
is a handsome man with blue eyes and black hair last week he was in paris
alistair usually visits paris in february

....

....

....

....

6 Zwei Rätsel

A

A Lösungshilfe

waagerecht **2** Can I have one of those ![jumper] please? (8)

3 His eyes are ...., not brown or blue. (5)

5 Are .... your glasses? (5)

7 He's very .... He's only fifteen. (5)

4 Two days after the ninth is the .... (8)

senkrecht **1** She .... plays squash
on Sundays. (7)

2 She types letters. She's a
.... (9)

6 Nine, ... eleven (3)

B Lösungshilfe

waagerecht **1** These are ![scissors] (8)

6 He is number one at the bank. He is the bank
.... (7)

7 My favourite sport is .... (6)

9 One box, two .... (5)

senkrecht **2** They were .... the drawer. (2)

3 Now they're .... the table. (2)

4 The cinema is in Green .... (6)

5 I usually .... at seven
o'clock in the morning. (4,2)

8 A new pair of ![shoes] . (5)

Interaction

1:

Look at the pictures. Put the words and phrases below in the right speech bubbles.

Excuse me.

The Arts Cinema?

(Thanks very much.) (Where can I see a good film?)

(Yes?) (You can try the Arts Cinema.)

(It's in Park Street opposite the supermarket.)

(Yes.) (Where's that?)

2:

Student **A**: Look at number 6 on page 78. Complete the chart by asking **B** questions.
Student **B**: Look at number 6 on page 84. Complete the chart by asking **A** questions.
Do not look at each other's charts until you have finished.

Does Tom like tennis?

Can Tom play baseball?

A   B

Listening and acting out 📼

1

Listen to the cassette and say whether the statements are true or false.

1 The man works in a theatre.
2 Miss Peabody is a secretary.
3 The man wants a secretary.

2

Listen to the cassette again. Complete this form.

NAME: ....

ABILITIES:	yes	no
Can type?	☐	☐
Can take shorthand?	☐	☐

OTHER ABILITIES

1 ....
2 ....
3 ....
4 ....

3

Have job interviews. Student **A** wants a job as a secretary and is interviewed by student **B**. **B** fills in the form based on **A'** abilities.

NAME:	yes	no
ABILITIES: Can type?	☐	☐
Can take shorthand?	☐	☐
What languages can he/she speak?	☐	☐

Language summary

Redewendungen		Neue Wörter	
Can Antonio type? – Yes, he can./No, he can't (= cannot).	Kann Antonio maschineschreiben? Ja./Nein.	angry ['æŋgri] beautiful ['bju:təful] paradise ['pærədaɪs] eat [i:t]	ärgerlich, böse schön Paradies essen
Where can I see a good film? – You can try the Studio Cinema.	Wo kann ich einen guten Film sehen? Du kannst/Sie können es mal im Studio Cinema versuchen.	top-class [tɒp'kla:s] king [kɪŋ] excellent ['eksələnt] play [pleɪ] only ['əʊnli]	erstklassig König ausgezeichnet spielen nur
You look tired. Do you want some help?	Du siehst/Sie sehen müde aus. Brauchst du/Brauchen Sie Hilfe?	modern ['mɒdən] shopping centre ['ʃɒpɪŋsentə] town [taʊn]	modern Einkaufszentrum Stadt
– I'll be all right.	Das wird schon wieder.	shorthand ['ʃɔ:thænd]	Kurzschrift

Grammatik

I	can		ich	kann
you	can		du	kannst/Sie können
he	can		er	kann
she	can		sie	kann
it	can		es	kann
we	can		wir	können
you	can		ihr	könnt/Sie können
they	can		sie	können

Das Hilfsverb *can* hat kein **s** in der dritten Person der Einzahl.

1 Wortschatz: geistige und körperliche Verfassung

Bilden Sie aus den angegebenen Buchstaben Wörter, die eine geistige oder körperliche Verfassung bezeichnen.

1 EHSEDAUXT   **2** GRAYN   **3** ERNVSOU   **4** DTRIE   **5** TSEPU   **6** IRODWRE

exhausted

2 can(not), do/does (not), am/is/are (not)

Setzen Sie die richtigen Wörter mit den richtigen Formen ein.

1 Can John play the piano? – Yes, he ....

2 Does he play the piano in the evenings? – No, he ....

3 Can he play the guitar? – Yes, he ....

4 Is John tall? – Yes, he ....

5 Does John like Indian food? – Yes, he ....

6 Are you English? – No, I ....

7 Can you speak French? – Yes, I ....

8 Do you play tennis? – Yes, we ....

9 Can you play the guitar? – Yes, I ....

3 can, can't

Schauen Sie sich die Tabelle an. Schreiben Sie dann fünf Sätze über die darin enthaltenen Informationen auf, wobei Sie *can* oder *can't* verwenden.

	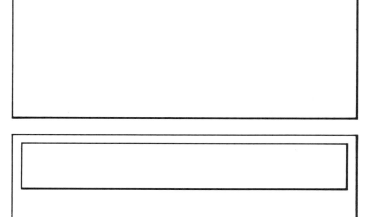			
MARK	✓	✗	✗	✗
KATIE	✗	✓	✗	✓
THE TWINS	✗	✗	✓	✓

1 ....

2 ....

3 ....

4 ....

5 ....

4 Lesen und schreiben Sie

COME TO BEAUTIFUL NORTHBOURNE!
The tourist's paradise!

- you can swim from the beaches
- you can eat at one of our top-class restaurants (for £15 you eat like a king)
- you can see excellent plays at the Majestic theatre or watch a good film at the Royal Cinema for only £3.00
- you can buy beautiful modern clothes at the new Kite Shopping Centre

NORTHBOURNE IS THE TOWN FOR YOU.
COME TODAY.

Schreiben Sie einen ähnlichen Text über Southbourne.

SOUTHBOURNE

- The Rainbow Gallery of Modern Art
- Greek food at the Athens Restaurant (£10 a person)
- The Arts Cinema
- The Midsummer Shopping Centre

Schreiben Sie einen ähnlichen Text über die Stadt, in der Sie wohnen.

12 Classwork

Interaction

1 ⦂⦂⦂

Team **A**: use this symbol, **O**
Team **B**: use this symbol, **X**
(*Note*: these symbols are called *noughts* and *crosses*.)

1 Choose a square.
2 Make a sentence with the word in the square.
3 Put your team's symbol in the square for a correct response.
4 The first team with a straight line of **0**s or **X**s wins.

always	can't	tall
his	leaves	mine
like	between	was

can	eyes	first
often	twice	were
opposite	onions	those

2 ⦂

Complete this questionnaire about your partner. Ask your partner how often he or she does the things and write the answers in the chart.

NAME: ....

AGE: ....

OCCUPATION: ....

FREQUENCY OF LEISURE ACTIVITIES

watch television ....

listen to music ....

read magazines ....

take exercise ....

play cards ....

play chess ....

go to a restaurant/bar ....

go to the cinema ....

Listening and acting out 📼

1

Listen to the cassette and answer the questions.

1 Who is Bud Samson?
2 Where are Terry and Bud?
3 What is Bud's hobby?
4 What is Bud's favourite food?

2

Listen to the cassette again. Put Bud's activities with the correct adverb.

always ....

often ....

usually ....

sometimes ....

3

In groups of three have interviews like the one on the cassette. Student **A** is a famous personality. Students **B** and **C** are reporters. They ask **A** about his/her activities, hobbies, likes and dislikes, etc.

Language summary

Redewendungen

What does Philip do on Saturdays?
– He always gets up before seven o'clock.

Was macht Philip Samstags?
Er steht immer vor sieben Uhr auf.

How often do you play football?
– About twice a week.

Wie oft spielst du/spielen Sie Fußball?
Ungefähr zweimal pro Woche.

Do you paint well?
– Not very well.
– Not too badly.

Malst du/malen Sie gut?
Nicht sehr gut.
Eigentlich ganz gut./Gar nicht so schlecht.

– Quite well.

Ziemlich gut.

Could you paint me a picture?
– All right.
– I'd rather not.

Könntest du/Könnten Sie ein Bild für mich malen?
In Ordnung.
Lieber nicht.

Neue Wörter

record ['rekɔːd] — Schallplatte
detective [dɪ'tektɪv] — Detektiv
colleague ['kɒliːg] — Kollege
lesson ['lesn] — (Unterrichts-)Stunde
sex [seks] — Geschlecht
leisure ['leʒə] — Muße
magazine [ˌmægə'ziːn] — Illustrierte
stamp [stæmp] — Briefmarke
fried egg [fraɪd 'eg] — Spiegelei
habit ['hæbɪt] — Angewohnheit

Grammatik

Adverbien der Häufigkeit (*usually, always, never, sometimes*) stehen vor dem Verb. Beispiel: *Peter usually goes to the cinema on Saturday evenings.*

---

1 Tätigkeiten

Verbinden Sie die folgenden Verben und Ausdrücke wie in Beispiel Nr.1.

1 drive	**a** French	**1**	*f*
2 cook	**b** a meal	**2**	
3 paint	**c** the piano	**3**	
4 type	**d** a letter	**4**	
5 sing	**e** awake	**5**	
6 read	**f** a car	**6**	
7 speak	**g** a picture	**7**	
8 give	**h** me a game	**8**	
9 play	**i** a song	**9**	
10 listen to	**j** television	**10**	
11 watch	**k** music	**11**	
12 stay	**l** a record	**12**	

2 what, where, what . . . like, how, how often

Setzen Sie das richtige Fragewort ein.

1 .... can I buy a stamp? – At the post office.

2 .... does Mabel travel to work? – By taxi.

3 .... does Mabel look ....? – She's a tall woman with blond hair and green eyes.

4 .... does Mabel go on holiday? – About four times a year.

5 .... is Mabel's house? – Near the station.

6 .... does Mabel have for breakfast? – Fried eggs.

7 .... does Mabel take exercise? – Never.

8 .... does Mabel do? – She's a businesswoman.

3 Wortstellung

Setzen Sie die Verben ins Präsens und das Adverb an die richtige Stelle.

Beispiel: **usually** Peter (go) to the cinema on Saturday evenings
Peter usually goes to the cinema on Saturday evenings.

1 always Peter (have) coffee for breakfast

....

2 usually Mary and Emma (go) to Spanish classes on Tuesdays and Thursc

....

3 never Peter (get) to work late

....

4 usually Mary and Emma (watch) the news on television

....

5 sometimes Peter (play) darts on Friday evenings

....

4 Satzzeichen und Großschreibung

Schreiben Sie die folgenden Sätze ab, und setzen Sie Großbuchstaben, Punkte und Fragezeichen, wo es nötig ist.

Beispiel: does simon play the guitar well
Does Simon play the guitar well?

1 where do mary and emma have lunch on sundays

....

2 you can see a good play at the majestic theatre

....

3 which is the platform for london

....

4 i usually eat at the mayfair restaurant

....

5 do i like paella yes i like it very much

....

5 Was tun Sie wie oft?

Ergänzen Sie die folgenden Sätze über sich selbst.

1 On Sundays I ....

2 Every Monday I ....

3 I .... once or twice a week.

4 I usually .... in the evening.

5 I always ....

---

6 Lesen und schreiben Sie

NAME:	Teresa Branco
AGE:	45
DESCRIPTION:	She is a tall, thin woman with long black hair and brown eyes.
HABITS:	She goes to the tennis club three times a week and she has lessons from Manuel da Silva. Mrs Branco plays tennis well. She always has lunch at the Caravela restaurant with her friend Emilia on Fridays. She sometimes has lunch at the tennis club with Jorge de Sousa. She never speaks to the manager of the club (Fernando Soares): they are not friends.

👀
EE
Detective
Agency

SIGNED: ....

Schauen Sie sich die folgenden Informationen über Teresas Ehemann an, und füllen Sie dann das Formular aus.

Julio Branco . . . 56 . . . tall . . . grey hair, blue eyes . . . office every day
. . . sauna twice a week . . . once a week squash with a colleague . . .
badly . . . once a week squash with his secretary . . . sometimes lunch
with his secretary . . . usually goes to work by car

NAME:

AGE:

DESCRIPTION:

👀
EE
Detective
Agency

HABITS:

SIGNED: ....

Interaction

1 ⁚⁚

In this mime game one student mimes an action; the others have to guess what it is. The student who guesses correctly gets a point. At the end of the game the student with the most points wins.

Are you reading a book?

No, I'm not.

Are you reading a newspaper?

Yes, I am.

2 ⁚

Student **A**: Look at number 7 on page 78. Complete the chart by asking **B** questions.
Student **B**: Look at number 7 on page 84. Complete the chart by asking **A** questions.
Do not look at each other's charts until you have finished.

What does Keith do?

He's a painter.

Listening and acting out 🔲

1

Listen to the cassette and answer the questions.

1 Where is Judith?
2 Who is paying for the call?
3 How is George feeling?
4 What is George doing?

2

Put the correct names, Tony, Jane, Martin and George under the pictures.

....

3

Student **A** rings home. Student **A** asks student **B**:
  how she/he is feeling
  how the other people in the house are
  what they are doing

Language summary

Redewendungen

What's (= What is) Mike doing?
– He's (= He is) making coffee.

Was macht Mike gerade/ jetzt?
Er macht gerade/jetzt Kaffee.

What are Ron and Kate doing?
– They're (= They are) peeling potatoes.

Was machen Ron und Kate gerade/jetzt?
Sie schälen gerade/jetzt Kartoffeln.

Is she nursing right now?
– Yes, she is./No, she isn't.

Arbeitet sie im Augenblick als Krankenschwester?
Ja./Nein.

Are they acting right now?

– Yes, they are./No, they aren't.

Spielen sie gerade/jetzt (Theater)?
Ja./Nein.

What's the matter? Why don't you take it to a vet?

– Perhaps I will.

Was ist los? Warum bringst du/bringen Sie sie/ ihn nicht zum Tierarzt?
Vielleicht tue ich es.

Neue Wörter

pay [peɪ]   bezahlen
call [kɔːl]   (Telefon-)Anruf
act [ækt]   eine Rolle spielen
sea [siː]   See, Meer
ghost [gəʊst]   Geist, Gespenst

Grammatik

I	am sailing	ich segle gerade
you	are sailing	du segelst gerade/ Sie segeln gerade
he	is sailing	er segelt gerade
she	is sailing	sie segelt gerade
it	is sailing	es segelt gerade
we	are sailing	wir segeln gerade
you	are sailing	ihr segelt gerade/ Sie segeln gerade
they	are sailing	sie segeln gerade

Die -ing Form bezeichnet einen Vorgang, der zu einem bestimmten Zeitpunkt gerade abläuft.

Die Normal-Form bezeichnet einen Vorgang, der für gewöhnlich oder immer so abläuft.

1 Wortschatz: Kochen

Finden Sie fünf Verben und zwei Substantiv aus dem Bereich ''Kochen'', und kreisen Sie sie ein wie im Beispiel.

t	a	s	t	i	n	g	c	h
o	a	b	c	a	e	f	h	i
m	p	c	g	h	i	j	o	j
a	e	o	k	l	m	n	p	k
t	e	o	o	p	q	r	p	l
o	l	k	s	t	u	v	i	m
w	i	i	f	r	y	i	n	g
x	n	n	y	z	a	b	g	n
e	g	g	c	d	e	f	g	o

2 do/does, is/are —ing

Welche Frage paßt zu welcher Antwort?

1 What does Tom do?	**a** No, he isn't	**1** ...... *f* ......
2 Is Steve teaching right now?	**b** He acts in plays.	**2** ....
3 How does Mary get to work?	**c** Yes, she does.	**3** ....
4 What does Steve teach?	**d** Yes, he is. He's playing Hamlet.	**4** ....
5 What is Mary doing right now?	**e** She drives her car.	**5** ....
6 Is Tom acting at this moment?	**f** He teaches English.	**6** ....
7 Does Mary drive a bus?	**g** She's driving her bus.	**7** ....

3 is/are —ing

Setzen Sie die jeweils richtige Verbform ein.

Beispiel: He (*not paint*) _isn't painting_ right now.

1 Steve (*swim*) .... in the sea right now.

2 Tom and Nigel (*not climb*) .... right now.

They (*have*) .... breakfast.

3 Joan (*make*) .... coffee right now.

She (*not swim*) .... with Steve.

4 Mary (*sail*) .... in the Caribbean right now.

She (*not drive*) .... her bus.

5 Chris and Sharon (*not watch*) .... a film right now.

They (*listen to*) .... the radio.

6 Steve (*not teach*) .... right now.

4 Zur Wiederholung

Wählen Sie die richtige Möglichkeit aus (*a* oder *b*).

Beispiel: I **a** were / **b** was in London. ...... *b* ......

1 What's John like? He's a **a** tall man. / **b** man tall. ....

2 John **a** work / **b** works in an office. ....

3 The post office is **a** next / **b** next to the station. ....

4 John can **a** swims. / **b** swim. ....

5 I **a** watch usually / **b** usually watch television. ....

5 Bildbeschreibung und Kommentar

Schreiben Sie einen Text über jede der beiden Zeichnungen.
Was passiert gerade? Was können Sie über die Personen sagen?

In the first picture ....

....

....

....

....

In the second picture ....

....

....

....

....

Interaction

1 ::

Look at the photographs and discuss them like the policemen. Say what you think the people are doing and what they have got in their hands, etc. You can see the photographs better on page 87.

What's the old woman doing?

She's watching television, I think.

What has she got in her hand?

A cigarette, I think.

2 ::

Ask students questions to complete the chart.

FIND SOMEONE WHO:

a was at a film yesterday evening ....

b can't play chess ....

c doesn't like classical music ....

d has got two brothers ....

e sometimes plays the guitar ....

f hasn't got a dog ....

g likes ice cream ....

h always has coffee for breakfast ....

i wasn't at home yesterday afternoon ....

j has got a car ....

Listening and acting out 🔘

1

Listen to the cassette and choose the correct answer **a**, **b** or **c**.

1 Maggie and John are in   **a** Mexico City.
                                   b Acapulco.
                                   c London.

2 Maggie wants   **a** vegetable soup.
                         b gazpacho.
                         c mushroom soup.

3 Today is   **a** Maggie's birthday.
                 b John's birthday.
                 c the waiter's birthday.

2

Listen to the cassette again. Answer the questions.

1 Does Maggie like the restaurant?
2 What is the date of Maggie's birthday?
3 Where did John see the date of Maggie's birthday?
4 What does John ask Maggie?

3

You are at a restaurant with a friend. Find out what your friend wants and then give the order to the waiter.
Ask your friend how he or she is getting on, etc.
Have a good meal!

Language summary

Redewendungen

Has the man got a passport/any gloves in his briefcase? – Yes, he has./No, he hasn't (= has not).	Hat der Mann einen Paß/Handschuhe in seiner Aktentasche? Ja./Nein.
What have you got in your bag? – I've (= I have) got my matches.	Was hast du/haben Sie in in deiner/Ihrer Tasche? Darin habe ich meine Streichhölzer.
They haven't got any glue but they've got some sellotape.	Sie haben keinen Klebstoff, aber sie haben Tesafilm.
Would you like some tea?	Möchtest du/Möchten Sie Tee?
– I'd prefer some coffee, if you've got any.	Iche möchte lieber Kaffee, wenn du welchen hast/Sie welchen haben.
How do you take it?	Wie hättest du/hätten Sie ihn gern?

Neue Wörter

hand [hænd]	Hand
soup [suːp]	Suppe
marry ['mæri]	heiraten
die [daɪ]	sterben
us [ʌs]	uns
hut [hʌt]	Hütte
snow [snəʊ]	Schnee
snowmobile ['snəʊməʊbiːl]	Schneemobil
broken ['brəʊkən]	zerbrochen
use [juːz]	gebrauchen
heating oil ['hiːtɪŋɔɪl]	Heizöl
fresh [freʃ]	frisch

Grammatik

I have got you have got he has got she has got it has got we have got you have got they have got	ich habe du hast/Sie haben … Die Form *got* dient nur der Verstärkung und wird nicht übersetzt.

some und *any*

Bei einer unbestimmten Menge kann das Substantiv im Englischen nicht (wie im Deutschen) allein stehen. Beachten Sie folgende Regeln:

Some steht in bejahten Aussagesätzen und in Fragen, wenn man eine positive Antwort erwartet.
Any steht in Fragen und verneinten Aussagesätzen. In bejahten Aussagesätzen hat es die Bedeutung "jede(r/s) beliebige".

Wortstellung

Im Deutschen wird durch die Fälle (z.B. Nominativ, Akkusativ) deutlich, wer was tut:
Der Hund beißt *den* Mann. ____ *Den* Mann beißt *der* Hund.
Wir können deshalb die Satzteile einfach vertauschen.
Versuchen wir das gleiche im Englischen:
The dog bites *the* man. ____ *The* man bites *the* dog.
Es geht nicht! Im zweiten Satz beißt der Mann den Hund.

Weil es keine Deklinationen im Englischen gibt, ist die Wortstellung strikt festgelegt:

Fragewort	(Hilfsverb)	Subjekt	Verb	Rest
1)		I	was	in Hong Kong yesterday.
2) Where	can	I	buy	a newspaper?

1) = Aussagesatz   2) = Fragesatz

---

1 Wortfeld: Essen

Setzen Sie die folgenden Wörter in die richtige Spalte. Fügen Sie weitere Wörter hinzu, wenn Sie können.

aubergines   omelette   butter
spaghetti   roast beef   cheese
steak   potatoes   onions
peppers   minced meat

Vegetable	Egg	Milk	Meat	Pasta
aubergines				

2 some, any

Setzen Sie das richtige Wort ein.

1 The bookshop has not got .... newspapers.

2 The man has got .... cigarettes in his briefcase.

3 Has the woman got .... cigarettes in her handbag?

4 They have not got .... pencils in the stationery shop.

5 Have they got .... ballpoint pens?

6 They have got .... correcting fluid.

3 Wortstellung

Ordnen Sie die Kästchen so, daß korrekte Sätze entstehen.
Setzen Sie Großbuchstaben, wo sie nötig sind.

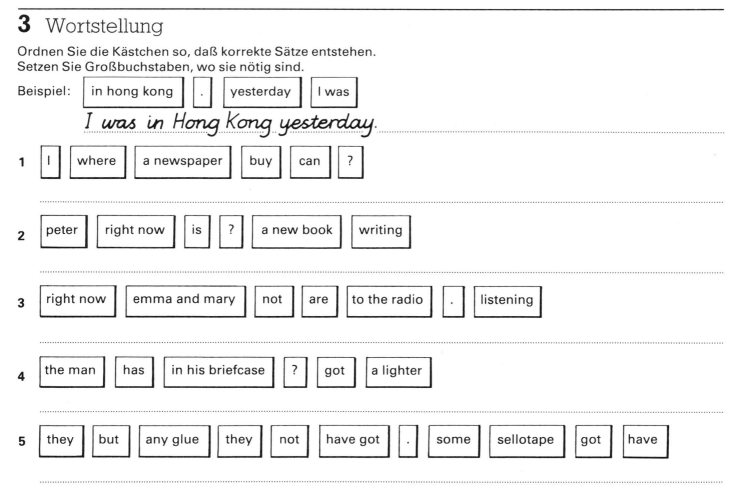

Beispiel: | in hong kong | . | yesterday | I was |

I was in Hong Kong yesterday.

1 | I | where | a newspaper | buy | can | ? |

2 | peter | right now | is | ? | a new book | writing |

3 | right now | emma and mary | not | are | to the radio | . | listening |

4 | the man | has | in his briefcase | ? | got | a lighter |

5 | they | but | any glue | they | not | have got | . | some | sellotape | got | have |

4 Bildbeschreibung

Notieren Sie fünf Sätze über die Bilder. Schreiben Sie, wie die Personen
aussehen und was sie haben (benutzen Sie *have got*).

1 ....
2 ....
3 ....
4 ....
5 ....

5 Lesen und schreiben Sie

Sie sind auf einer verlassenen Insel.
Sie wollen einen Hilferuf per
Flaschenpost abschicken. Hier sind
ein paar Stichwörter, die Ihnen
helfen können. Schreiben Sie,
bevor es zu spät ist!

small island . . . dying . . . no food
. . . some fresh water . . . all lying
under the trees . . . very weak . . .

15 Classwork

Interaction

1:

In pairs put the following sentences in the correct order to make a dialogue. (The first one is done for you.)

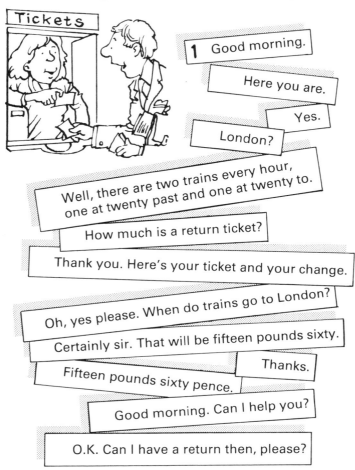

1 Good morning.

Here you are.

Yes.

London?

Well, there are two trains every hour, one at twenty past and one at twenty to.

How much is a return ticket?

Thank you. Here's your ticket and your change.

Oh, yes please. When do trains go to London?

Certainly sir. That will be fifteen pounds sixty.

Fifteen pounds sixty pence.

Thanks.

Good morning. Can I help you?

O.K. Can I have a return then, please?

2:

Student **A**: Look at number 8 on page 79.
Complete the chart by asking student **B**.
Student **B**: Look at number 8 on page 85.
Complete the chart by asking student **A**.
Do not look at each other's charts until you have finished.

How much tea is there in the shop?

How many potatoes are there in the shop?

Listening and acting out 📼

1

Listen to the cassette and answer the questions.

1 Who is selling the house, the man or the woman?
2 How many rooms has the house got?
3 How much is the house, according to the newspaper?
4 How much is the house, according to the woman?

2

Listen to the cassette again and write the correct numbers.

Bedrooms ....

Bathrooms ....

Acres (*of land*) ....

Swimming pools ....

3

Student **B** is selling his/her house.
Student **A** wants information about the house.
Student **A** rings up student **B**. Student **A** should ask about the numbers of bedrooms/bathrooms, etc.

Language summary

Redewendungen

Are there any rivers in the Isle of Man?
– Yes, there are four./No, there aren't (= are not).

Is there any agriculture in the Isle of Man?
– Yes, there is./No, there isn't (= is not).

How many tomatoes are there?
– There are a lot/aren't many/aren't any.

How much sugar is there?
– There is a lot/isn't much/isn't any.

I'd like a ticket for eight o'clock.
– Let's see. That's fine. Will you pay by cheque or in cash?

Gibt es Flüsse auf der Insel Man?
Ja, (es gibt) vier./Nein, (es gibt) keine.

Gibt es Landwirtschaft auf der Insel Man?
Ja./Nein.

Wie viele Tomaten sind da?
Es sind viele/nicht viele/gar keine da.

Wieviel Zucker ist da?
Es ist viel/nicht viel/gar keiner da.

Ich hätte gern eine Karte für acht Uhr.
Sehen wir mal nach. Das geht. Zahlen Sie mit Scheck oder bar?

Neue Wörter

acre ['eɪkə]	"Morgen", eine Fläche von 4046, 8 qm
land [lænd]	Land
natural resources ['nætʃrəl rɪ'sɔːsɪz]	Bodenschätze
energy ['enədʒi]	Energie
industrial [ɪn'dʌstrɪəl]	industriell
nation ['neɪʃn]	Nation
according to [ə'kɔːdɪŋ tuː]	entsprechend
adventure [əd'ventʃə]	Abenteuer
fridge [frɪdʒ]	Kühlschrank
rich [rɪtʃ]	reich
over ['əʊvə]	über
important [ɪm'pɔːtənt]	wichtig
possible ['pʊsəbəl]	möglich
such [sʌtʃ]	solch
serious ['sɪərɪəs]	ernst
unemployed [ˌʌnem'plɔɪd]	arbeitslos
business ['bɪznɪs]	Geschäft
close [kləʊz]	schließen
Scotland ['skɒtlənd]	Schottland
Northern Ireland ['nɔːðn 'aɪələnd]	Nordirland

1 Wortfeld: Geographie

Schauen Sie sich die Karte an, und setzen Sie dann die Wörter auf die richtigen Zeilen.

airport
oil
village
town
bridge
mountain
coal
river
factory

village

2 Zur Wiederholung

Verbinden Sie die folgenden Fragen mit den richtigen Antworten wie in Beispiel Nr. 1.

1 Have you got any paper clips?	**a** I go swimming.	**1** _h_
2 How much chalk is there?	**b** About twice a week.	**2** ....
3 Are there any rivers in the Isle of Man?	**c** I like adventure films best.	**3** ....
4 How often do you play squash?	**d** Yes, there is.	**4** ....
5 What do you do on Sundays?	**e** At the newsagent's.	**5** ....
6 How many brothers have you got?	**f** Yes, I can.	**6** ....
7 Where can I buy a newspaper?	**g** Two.	**7** ....
8 What's your favourite kind of film?	**h** No, I haven't.	**8** ....
9 Is there any agriculture near your town?	**i** Yes, there are four.	**9** ....
10 Can you play chess?	**j** There are three boxes.	**10** ....

3 there is, there are

Setzen Sie das richtige Wort ein.

1 There .... some cheese on the table.

2 .... there any sausages in the supermarket?

3 There .... five kilos of tomatoes in the kitchen.

4 .... there any margarine in the fridge?

5 There .... not any honey in the grocery.

4 how much, how many

Setzen Sie die richtigen Wörter ein.

1 .... sisters have you got?

2 .... orange juice is there on the table?

3 .... petrol is there in the car?

4 .... erasers have you got?

5 .... cars can you see?

5 there is/there are, has got/have got

Lesen Sie den Abschnitt, und setzen Sie nur jeweils ein Wort ein.

The United Kingdom consists of England, Scotland, Northern Ireland and Wales. The UK [1]..................... got a population of about 60 million. The UK is very rich in natural energy resources. There [2]..................... a lot of oil in the North Sea and [3]..................... lot of coal all over Britain (England, Scotland and Wales). The UK is an industrial nation but it has [4]..................... serious problems. [5]..................... are over four million unemployed, and many businesses are closing.

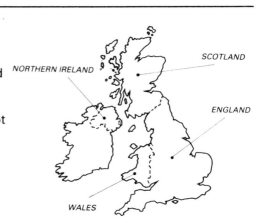

6 Lesen und schreiben Sie

Schauen Sie sich die Karte und die dazugehörigen
Informationen an. Schreiben Sie dann einen Text
über das Land.

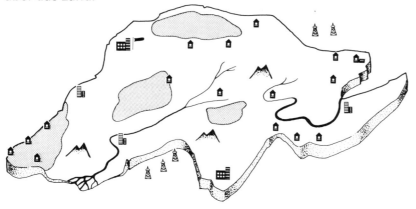

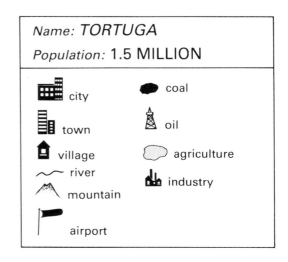

Name: **TORTUGA**

Population: 1.5 MILLION

city

town

village

river

mountain

airport

coal

oil

agriculture

industry

....

....

....

....

....

Schreiben Sie jetzt einen ähnlichen Text über Ihr eigenes Land.

Interaction

1:

Fill in the calendar about your partner's activities next week. Ask what he or she is going to do and record the answers.

MONDAY	morning	
	afternoon	
	evening	
TUESDAY	morning	
	afternoon	
	evening	
WEDNESDAY	morning	
	afternoon	
	evening	
THURSDAY	morning	
	afternoon	
	evening	
FRIDAY	morning	
	afternoon	
	evening	

2::

Look at the photographs and discuss them like the policemen. Say who you think the people are, what they have got and what they are going to do. You can see the photographs better on page 88.

What's the girl going to do?

What can you see in the picture of the man?

Listening and acting out 📼

1

Listen to the cassette and answer the questions.

1 Who is Ernest B. Gold?
2 When is the shuttle going to lift off?
3 What is the main objective of the mission?
4 What does Steve Terelli do well?

2

Complete the mission details.

```
MISSION DETAILS
Number of crew members: Men: _____

                      Women: _____

Main Objective: to  _____ supplies

Other tasks:

1 _____ radiation levels

2 _____ the moon
```

3

Student **A** is going on an expedition to either **a** the North Pole, or **b** the sea bed, or **c** a deserted island.
Student **A** plans who is going to go on the expedition and what they are going to do.
Student **B** interviews student **A** about the expedition.

Language summary

Redewendungen

What's (= What is) Tom going to do in March?
– He's (= He is) going to get married.

Was wird Tom im März machen?
Er wird heiraten.

Why is Neil wearing a spacesuit?
– Because he's going to walk in space.

Warum trägt Neil einen Raumanzug?
Weil er einen Weltraum-spaziergang machen will.

Where are you off to?

Wo willst du/wollen Sie hin?

You'd better take light clothes.

Du solltest/Sie sollten lieber leichte Kleidung mitnehmen.

Grammatik

What am I	going to do?	Was werde /will ich tun?
What are you	going to do?	Was wirst /willst du tun?
		Was werden/wollen Sie tun?
What is he	going to do?	Was wird /will er tun?
What is she	going to do?	Was wird /will sie tun?
What is it	going to do?	Was wird /will es tun?
What are we	going to do?	Was werden/wollen wir tun?
What are you	going to do?	Was werden/wollt ihr tun?
		Was werden/wollen Sie tun?
What are they	going to do?	Was werden/wollen sie tun?

Neue Wörter

director [dɪˈrektə]	Direktor
shuttle [ˈʃʌtəl]	Raumfähre
lift off [lɪft ˈɒf]	abheben
main objective [meɪn əbˈdʒektɪv]	Hauptziel
crew [kruː]	Mannschaft
member [ˈmembə]	Mitglied
departure [dɪˈpɑːtʃə]	Abflug
university [juːnɪˈvɜːsəti]	Universität
telephone [ˈtelɪfəʊn]	Telefon
family [ˈfæməli]	Familie
sky [skaɪ]	Himmel
deliver [dɪˈlɪvə]	liefern
supplies [səˈplaɪz]	Nachschub
radiation level [ˌreɪdɪˈeɪʃn ˈlevəl]	Strahlungsintensität
moon [muːn]	Mond
all [ɔːl]	alle
chaotic [keɪˈɒtɪk]	chaotisch
change [tʃeɪndʒ]	wechseln
job [dʒɒb]	Arbeitsplatz
later [ˈleɪtə]	später
write [raɪt]	schreiben

Der Ausdruck *going to* mit der Grundform des Verbs wird verwendet, wenn wir eine Absicht, einen bereits gefaßten Plan ausdrücken wollen.

1 Wortfeld: Kleidungsstücke

Schreiben Sie die Wörter aus der Liste in die richtige Spalte. In Spalte 1 z.B. stehen alle Kleidungsstücke, die man auf dem Kopf tragen kann.
Manche Wörter können in verschiedenen Spalten gleichzeitig stehen.

shorts
leotard
apron
anorak
skirt
sweater
jacket
shirt
dress

trousers
shoes
glasses
hat
coat
gloves
crash helmet
boots
suit

1 _____

2 _____

3 _____

4 _____

5 _____

6 _____

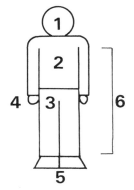

2 going to, is —ing

Setzen Sie die richtige Form ein.

Example: Carmen (*wash*) ......*is washing*...... her hair right now.

1 Right now Carmen (*watch*) .... television at home.

2 Next Monday she (*see*) .... a new film with her boyfriend.

3 In May she (*travel*) .... to England.

4 In May, June and July next summer she (*study*) .... at an English university.

5 Now she (*talk*) .... to her boyfriend on the telephone.

6 Tomorrow morning she (*drive*) .... to her sister's house.

7 Tomorrow afternoon she (*play*) .... tennis with her sister.

8 Carmen's sister (*play*) .... the piano at a concert right now.

9 Right now Carmen's father (*wash*) .... the dishes.

10 Carmen (*cook*) .... a meal for the family next Sunday.

3 Wortstellung

Ordnen Sie die Kästchen so, daß korrekte Sätze entstehen.
Setzen Sie Großbuchstaben, wo es nötig ist.

Beispiel: | in hong kong | | yesterday | I was |

I was in Hong Kong yesterday.

1 | the piano | the guitar | . | can play | antonio | can't play | but | he |
....

2 | in | any butter | is | the fridge | ? | there |
....

3 | florida | peter | . | next july | to visit | is going |
....

4 | industry | the isle of man | ? | how much | there | is | in |
....

5 | mary and emma | spanish classes | go to | how often | ? | do |
....

4 Ein Gespräch

Ergänzen Sie den Dialog.

A: Where **1**.................................... off to?

B: **2**.................................... buy a newspaper.

A: You **3**.................................... take an umbrella.

B: Why?

A: Look at the sky! It **4**.................................... rain.

B: I know. But I **5**.................................... walk to the shop, I'm going to drive!

A: Oh! **6**.................................... buy a newspaper for me?

B: Yes, of course. Which is your **7**.................................... newspaper?

A: I **8**.................................... The Guardian **9**....................................

B: Yes, I like The Guardian **10**.................................... . I'll get you one.

5 going to

Ergänzen Sie die folgenden Sätze über sich selbst.

1 On Sunday I ....

2 I .... by car tomorrow.

3 I .... in July.

4 .... cook a meal.

5 In five minutes from now ....

6 Lesen und schreiben Sie

2126 Atlantic Drive
NY 656
USA

Dear Mum,

Thank you for your letter. We are all well here.

Next month is going to be chaotic! Peter is going to change his job on the 5th and he is going to fly to Europe a week later (the 12th). Roger is going to start at his new school next Monday. We are a bit worried. Is he going to like it ??!!

I'll write again soon. Love to Dad,

Lucy

Mrs G. Cunningham
3 Parsonage Street
Oxford
England

Schreiben Sie einen ähnlichen Brief an eine(n) englische(n) Freund(in). Berichten Sie, was Sie und Ihre Familie in naher Zukunft vorhaben.

17 Classwork

Interaction

1 ∴
Ask other students questions to complete the chart.

> **FIND SOMEONE WHO:**
>
> **1** took a photograph last week ....
>
> **2** fried an egg last weekend ....
>
> **3** wore a suit two days ago ....
>
> **4** went camping last year ....
>
> **5** collects stamps ....
>
> **6** always reads in bed ....
>
> **7** is going to watch television tonight ....

2 :

a Put the sentences in the correct order to make a dialogue. The first one is done for you.

What have you got in your hand?

> **1** What have you got in your hand?

> For the film festival.

> Why are you going to go there?

> An airline ticket to Paris.

> Do you always go to the Paris festival?

> I bought a motorbike and drove to Montpellier in June.

> No. Last year I didn't go to any festivals.

> What did you do?

b Fill in these charts about the girl's two journeys with information from the dialogue.

LAST YEAR	THIS YEAR
Destination:	Destination:
Reason:	Reason:
Means of transport:	Means of transport:

Listening and acting out 📼

1
Listen to the cassette and put these pictures (**a–f**) in the correct order in the box below.

1	2	3	4	5	6

2
Answer the questions.

1 What did Mrs Jones buy at the chemist's?

2 What was the car like?

3 How many men were there in the car
  a when it arrived? **b** when it drove away?

4 Why did the man with glasses fall down?

5 What did Mrs Jones do?

3
Student **A** saw the robbery. Student **B** is the policeman.
Student **A** tells the policeman about the robbery.

Language summary

<table>
<tr><td>

Redewendungen

What did Sofia do on
Monday morning?
– She went shopping.

Did Jane write a report?

– Yes, she did./No, she
didn't (= did not).
What did she write,
then?

What did you think of the
play?
– I thought it was boring.
– So did I.
– I didn't. I thought it was
good.

</td><td>

Was hat Sofia Montag
morgen gemacht?
Sie war einkaufen.

Hat Jane einen Bericht
geschrieben?
Ja./Nein.

Was hat sie denn
geschrieben?

Wie fandest du/fanden Sie
das Stück?
Ich fand, es war langweilig.
Ich auch.
Ich nicht. Ich fand, es war
gut.

</td></tr>
</table>

Neue Wörter

camp [kæmp]	zelten
collect [kə'lekt]	sammeln
rail [reɪl]	Bahn
reason ['riːzən]	Grund
means of transport	Transportmittel
[miːnz əv'trænspɔːt]	
drive away [,draɪv ə'weɪ]	wegfahren
robbery ['rɒbəri]	Raub
bowl [bəʊl]	Schüssel
tennis player ['tenɪspleɪə]	Tennisspieler
arm [ɑːm]	Arm
ladder ['lædə]	Leiter
fall down [fɔːl'daʊn]	hinunterfallen
plaster ['plɑːstə]	Gips
take off [,teɪk'ɒf]	abnehmen
dizzy ['dɪzi]	schwindlig
faint [feɪnt]	in Ohnmacht fallen

Grammatik

Verben bilden die Vergangenheitsform (past simple)
entweder durch Anhängen der Endung -ed (= regelmäßig)
oder durch eine eigene Form (= unregelmäßig).

regelmäßige Verben		unregelmäßige Verben	
Gegenwart	*Vergangenheit*	*Gegenwart*	*Vergangenheit*
happen	happened	do	did
push	pushed	put	put
scream	screamed	drive	drove
stop	stopped	get	got
listen	listened	throw	threw
visit	visited	buy	bought
cook	cooked	go	went
watch	watched	read	read
look	looked	think	thought

Im Deutschen verwenden wir oft Perfektformen, um über
vergangene, abgeschlossene Ereignisse zu sprechen
(siehe das Beispiel unten). Das ist im Englischen *nicht*
möglich: Vergangene, abgeschlossene Ereignisse
erfordern die Vergangenheit (past tense).

Frage				*Antwort*	
What did	**I**	**do?**		**I**	**screamed.**
Was habe	ich	getan?		Ich	habe geschrien.
What did	**you**	**do?**		**You**	**screamed.**
Was hast	du	getan?		Du	hast geschrien./
Was haben	Sie	getan?		Sie	haben geschrien.
What did	**he**	**do?**		**He**	**screamed.**
Was hat	er	getan?		Er	hat geschrien.
What did	**she**	**do?**		**She**	**screamed.**
Was hat	sie	getan?		Sie	hat geschrien.
What did	**it**	**do?**		**It**	**screamed.**
Was hat	es	getan?		Es	hat geschrien.
What did	**we**	**do?**		**We**	**screamed.**
Was hat	wir	getan?		Wir	haben geschrien.
What did	**you**	**do?**		**You**	**screamed.**
Was habt	ihr	getan?		Ihr	habt geschrien./
Was haben	Sie	getan?		Sie	haben geschrien.
What did	**they do?**			**They screamed.**	
Was haben	sie	getan?		Sie	haben geschrien.

Fragen werden in der Vergangenheit mit *did*
(= Vergangenheitsform von *do*) + Grundform gebildet.

1 Vergangenheit und Gegenwart

Setzen Sie die richtige Zeitform
des Verbs ein.

Beispiel: Yesterday I (go) .... *went* .... to the shops.

1 Every day Jane (go) .... to work by car.

2 Yesterday morning she (get) .... up late.

3 Jane's car (not start) .... yesterday morning.

4 Jane usually (have) .... lunch in the hospital canteen.

5 Yesterday she (have) .... lunch with her father in a restaurant.

6 Last week Jane and her boyfriend, Antonio, (buy) .... a new car.

7 Last Wednesday they (drive) .... to a village for lunch.

8 Jane sometimes (cook) .... a meal for Antonio.

9 Last night she (make) .... a fantastic paella.

2 Fragen in der Vergangenheitsform

Ergänzen Sie die folgenden Fragen über Jenny.

1 Where ....? – She went to the cinema.

2 What .... last night? – She cooked moussaka.

3 What .... this morning? – She read the newspaper.

4 .... on television yesterday? – She watched the news.

5 .... to work? – She ran because she was late.

3 Zur Wiederholung

Wählen Sie die richtige Möglichkeit aus (a oder b).

Beispiel: I **a** were / **b** was in London. ..... *b* .....

1 Do you like football? Yes, I **a** like. / **b** do. ....

2 What is John doing? He **a** is watching / **b** watching television. ....

3 There **a** is / **b** are some sugar in the bowl. ....

4 How much **a** the pen is? / **b** is the pen? Forty-nine pence. ....

5 What **a** do / **b** does you do on Sundays? I go jogging. ....

4 Zur Wiederholung

Lesen Sie die folgende Geschichte, und setzen Sie jeweils ein Wort in die Lücken.

Jimmy is a tennis player. He did [1] .... play tennis today

because he [2] .... his arm two weeks ago. He was on a ladder

in [3] .... town library. He took a [4] .... from the

shelf but he fell down. A friend [5] .... him to the hospital and

they put his [6] .... in plaster. Jimmy was in hospital for a

week. He [7] .... television and listened to the radio.

[8] .... thought it was very boring.

   Now Jimmy is at home again, but he is not [9] .... to play

tennis for four weeks. They are going [10] .... take the plaster

off next Wednesday.

5 Lesen und schreiben Sie

Letzten Freitag hat Sofia Menotti aus Padua ihre Großmutter in Verona besucht. Schauen Sie sich die Bilder an, und schreiben Sie die Geschichte zu Ende.

Die folgenden Ausdrücke können Ihnen helfen: *open, say, watch, cook, stop, put petrol in the car*. Lassen Sie sich ein interessantes Ende einfallen.

....

....

....

....

....

....

....

....

18 Classwork

Interaction

1 :::

In two teams write ten general knowledge questions.
Now team **A** asks team **B** a question. Team **B** gets a
point if they can answer correctly. Then team **B** asks
team **A**. The team with the most points wins the game.

Who painted the Mona Lisa?

Why is Neil Armstrong famous?

When was Columbus born?

2 ::

a Group **A**: Look at number 9 on page 79.
Group **B**: Look at number 9 on page 85.
Group **C**: Look at number 9 on page 87.
Group **D**: Look at number 9 on page 88.
Each group should write two sentences about their
picture using the past tense. **A**

b Make new groups with students from groups **A**,
B, **C** and **D**. Tell the story in sequence *without
looking at the pictures.*

... the explorer in the jungle ...

... he fell to the ground ...

... she ran out of the house ...

... he saw an old temple ...

Listening and acting out 📼

1

Listen to the cassette and put these pictures (**a–d**)
in the correct order in the box below.

1	2	3	4

2

Answer the questions.

1 Who knocked on the door?
2 Who knocked the milk off the table?
3 Who ran into the road?
4 Who fell off her bicycle?
5 Who helped Janice off the ground?

3

Student **A** thinks of three things that happened that
made her/him late. Student **A** arrives at **B**'s house
late. **B** asks **A** what happened to her/him.

Language summary

Redewendungen

Who composed the Messiah? – G.F. Handel.	Wer hat den Messias komponiert? G.F. Händel.
Why is Edmund Hillary famous? – Because he climbed Mount Everest.	Warum ist Edmund Hillary berühmt? Weil er den Mount Everest bestiegen hat.
When was he born? – In 1919. – I've no idea.	Wann ist er geboren? 1919. Keine Ahnung!
I'm sorry I'm late.	Entschuldige/Entschuldigen Sie, daß ich zu spät komme.
– What happened to you?	Was war los?
Oh well! It doesn't matter. Not to worry.	Nun ja! Das macht nichts. Kein Grund zur Beunruhigung.

Neue Wörter

temple ['tempəl]	Tempel
bring [brɪŋ]	bringen
rope [rəʊp]	Seil
knock (on the door) ['nɒk (ɒn ðə 'dɔː)]	(an die Tür) klopfen
knock (the milk) off ['nɒk (ðə mɪlk) ɒf]	(die Milch) runterstoßen
bicycle ['baɪsɪkəl]	Fahrrad
plane [pleɪn]	Flugzeug
barrier ['bærɪə]	Barriere
come, came [kʌm, keɪm]	kommen, kam
customs hall ['kʌstəmzhɔːl]	Zollabfertigungshalle
shout [ʃaʊt]	laut rufen
shot [ʃɒt]	Schuß
cottage ['kɒtɪdʒ]	Hütte
door [dɔː]	Tür
bin [bɪn]	Mülleimer
sink [sɪŋk]	(Küchen-)Ausguß

Grammatik

Wenn das Fragewort nach dem Subjekt fragt, bleibt die Satzstellung des Aussagesatzes (Subjekt-Verb-Rest) erhalten.
Deshalb braucht man *keine* Form von *do*.
Beispiel: *Who composed the Messiah?*

Auch Fragesätze mit einem Hilfsverb (z.B. *is, was, have*) brauchen *keine* Form von *do*.
Beispiel: *Why is Edmund Hillary famous?*

Jahreszahlen stehen nicht allein, sondern werden mit *in* eingeführt. Beispiel: *That was in 1920* (lies: *in nineteen-twenty*).

1 Vergangenheitsformen regelmäßiger Verben

Schreiben Sie die Vergangenheitsformen der folgenden Verben entsprechend dem Klang ihrer Endungen in die richtige Spalte.

happen
scream
land
listen
compose
stop
visit
push
invent
discover
design
conquer
survive
save
kill
cook
watch

/d/	/t/	/ɪd/
happen - happened	push - pushed	visit - visited

2 Fragen und Antworten in der Vergangenheitsform

Verbinden Sie die folgenden Fragen und Antworten wie im Beispiel.

1 Who wrote Don Quixote?		**a** In 1564.		**1**	_C_
2 What did Columbus do in 1492?		**b** He wrote music.		**2**	
3 Why is Cervantes famous?		**c** Cervantes.		**3**	
4 Where did Napoleon die?		**d** Because he was president of the USA.		**4**	
5 When was Shakespeare born?		**e** No, he didn't.		**5**	
6 Did Lauren Bacall marry Humphrey Bogart?		**f** Michaelangelo.		**6**	
7 Did Shakespeare write Evita?		**g** On the island of Elba.		**7**	
8 Why is Kennedy famous?		**h** Because he wrote Don Quixote.		**8**	
9 Who painted the Sistine Chapel?		**i** He discovered America.		**9**	
10 What did Beethoven do?		**j** Yes, she did.		**10**	

3 Hilfsverben: be, do, can, have

Setzen Sie die richtigen Wörter in der richtigen Zeitform
(Vergangenheit oder Gegenwart) ein.

1 .... you going to visit your grandmother tomorrow? No, I'm not.

2 .... you play chess in the evenings? – Yes, sometimes.

3 .... you watch television last night? – No, I did not.

4 .... I buy a camera in this shop? – Yes, what kind would you like?

5 .... you got any films for the camera? – Yes.

6 .... Steve and Joan visit Germany? – No, they visited France and Spain.

7 .... Tom and Nigel climb mountains every year? – No, not always.

8 .... Antonio speak Portuguese? – Yes, of course.

9 .... Pedro go to the United States last year? – Yes, for three months.

10 .... you got any shorts? – Yes . . . blue and white ones.

4 Wortstellung

Ordnen Sie die Kästchen so, daß korrekte Sätze entstehen.
Setzen Sie Großbuchstaben, wo sie nötig sind.

Beispiel: | in hong kong | | yesterday | | . | | I was |

I was in Hong Kong yesterday.

1 | to the cinema | | last night | | john | | ? | | go | | did |

....

2 | any cheese | | she has got | | . | | she has not got | | but | | some butter |

....

3 | in bed | but | not sleeping | . | atsuko | is | she is |

....

4 | sunday morning | john | last | do | what | ? | did |

....

5 | to the university | yesterday | carmen did not | , | she went | . | go to the beach |

....

5 Lesen und schreiben Sie

Lesen Sie den nebenstehenden Auszug aus Geoffrey Bridgers Buch *To Kill in Kowloon*.
Schauen Sie sich dann seine Notizen zum ersten Kapitel seines neuen Buches *To Kill at Home* an.
Benutzen Sie diese Notizen, und schreiben Sie den Anfang des Kapitels.

Chapter 1 – The Cottage

car – 11.30 p.m. – cottage
tall woman – blond hair
table – plate of spaghetti
spaghetti – plate – in the bin
made some coffee – watched TV
man looked through window
screamed

Chapter 1: The airport

At ten o'clock in the morning a plane landed at Kowloon airport and a tall man with fair hair and blue eyes got out and walked towards the airport buildings.

There was a beautiful Chinese girl at the barrier. She looked at all the passengers as they came out of the customs hall. Suddenly she screamed, 'Gregory, Gregory. I'm over here!' The tall man looked at her and ran towards her. 'My Ling,' he shouted.

There was a shot and the man fell to the ground.

19 Classwork

Interaction

1:

In pairs put the following cards in the correct order to make a dialogue. The first one is done for you.

1 Do you like your job?

Well anyway, would you like a cup of coffee?

It's exhausting. I have to wash the floors, clean the windows, empty the ashtrays . . .

No, I don't.

Oh, I don't know. I'd like to travel . . . and I want to study.

Why not?

No, I don't think so. I can't afford to.

Well what would you like to do instead?

Are you going to leave this job then?

Yes, please. That would be great!

2:

Complete the chart by interviewing your partner.

NAME: ....

AGE: ....

OCCUPATION: ....

OBLIGATIONS: ....

at home ....
at school/college/work

....

PLANS/AMBITIONS (what would he or she like to do in the future?):

....

Listening and acting out 🔊

1

Listen to the cassette and say whether the following statements are true or false.

1 Anne is an athlete.
2 Jo is a marathon runner.
3 Anne doesn't want to make a parachute jump.
4 Jo makes a parachute jump every day.

2

Listen to the cassette again and answer the questions.

1 How often does Anne train?
2 How far does Anne run in training?
3 When is the marathon race?
4 When is Jo's first jump?

3

In pairs have a similar conversation. Student **A** invites student **B**.
Student **B** says 'No . . . I have to . . .'
Student **A** tries to persuade student **B** (like Jo on the cassette). **B** continues to make excuses.

Language summary

Redewendungen

What does Lucy have to do?
– She has to make the beds.

What would Lucy like to do?
– She'd like to meet the president.

What's the matter with the man?
– He has to go to the office party but he doesn't want to meet the boss's wife.

Would you like to come for a drink?

– I can't, I'm afraid.
What about tomorrow?
– That would be great.

Was muß Lucy machen?

Sie muß die Betten machen.

Was würde Lucy gern tun?

Sie würde gern den Präsidenten kennenlernen.

Was ist los mit dem Mann?

Er muß zur Betriebsfeier, aber er möchte nicht mit der Frau des Chefs zusammentreffen.

Hättest du/Hätten Sie Lust, auf einen Drink vorbeizukommen?
Ich kann leider nicht.
Wie ist es morgen?
Das wäre prima.

Neue Wörter

afford [ə'fɔːd]   sich leisten
empty ['empti]   ausleeren
ashtray ['æʃtreɪ]   Aschenbecher
instead [ɪn'sted]   statt dessen
obligation [ˌɒblɪ'geɪʃn] Verpflichtung
ambition [æm'bɪʃn]   Ehrgeiz
marvellous ['mɑːvələs]   prima, wunderbar
enjoy yourself   amüsier dich/amüsieren
        [en'dʒɔɪ jɔː'self] Sie sich gut
smile [smaɪl]   lächeln
participate [pɑː'tɪsɪpeɪt] teilnehmen

Grammatik

have to wird in der Gegenwart wie *must* gebraucht; es weist aber darauf hin, daß der Zwang zum Handeln von außen kommt.

Nach *want* steht immer die *Grundform mit* **to**.

1 Typische Ausdrücke

Verbinden Sie die folgenden Verben und Ausdrücke wie im Beispiel.

1	wash	a	for a meal	1	_b_
2	answer	b	my hair	2	
3	make	c	exercise	3	
4	miss	d	the telephone	4	
5	take	e	Naples	5	
6	get	f	the bus	6	
7	visit	g	to Naples	7	
8	come	h	the beds	8	
9	drive	i	married	9	

2 Fragewörter: what, where, why, how, who, how often

Setzen Sie das richtige Fragewort ein.

1 .... is Dimitri wearing an apron? – He's going to cook a meal.

2 .... is Jane doing right now? – She's reading a medical journal.

3 .... does Mario play squash? – About once a week.

4 ....did Steve and Joan go to Spain? – By car.

5 .... got wet last night? – Atsuko did.

6 .... does Lucy play cards? – In the Bridge Club.

7 .... does Jane want to do? – She wants to get married.

8 .... does Dimitri watch television? – Every evening.

9 .... did Peter go last September? – To Acapulco.

3 have to, want to

Setzen Sie das Verb in seiner richtigen Form ein, und verbinden Sie es mit *want to* oder *have to*.

Beispiel: Jane (*get married*) *wants to get married* but Antonio does not.

1 Sylvie (*get up*) .... at six o'clock every morning. She does not like it.

2 Steve and Joan (*visit*) .... Turkey for their holiday next year.

3 Sofia (*learn*) .... Greek. She has got a Greek boyfriend.

4 Peter and Lucy (*go*) .... to a party tonight but they are not happy about it.

5 Caroline (*make*) .... beds at the hospital and she does not like it.

4 Zur Wiederholung

Setzen Sie in jede Lücke nur jeweils ein Wort ein.

Caroline Gordon is not happy **1**.. the hospital where she is

2.. nurse. She does not **3**.. the work and

she thinks **4**.. is boring. Every day she has

5.. make beds, feed the patients **6**.. write

reports. This afternoon Caroline **7**.. going to ring her

friend and **8**.. are going to talk about **9**..

holidays. Last year they went **10**.. the Alps but they

11.. not know where to go this year. **12**..

and her friend like climbing **13**.. Caroline climbs very well.

The only problem is that Caroline **14**.. go on a

15.. expensive holiday. She has not **16**.. a lot of

money.

At **17**.. moment Caroline is talking to **18**..

patient, but she is thinking about her **19**... She

20.. to leave the hospital right now, but she has still got two

hours left at work.

5 Lesen und schreiben Sie

Lesen Sie diese Anzeige:

Is your life boring? Are you always exhausted?

We can help you!

Listen to previous Club Aegean guests.

'I loved it! Club Aegean was exciting!'
Hilda Blank, London.

'It was fantastic! Lots of sun.'
Jeff Tomson, Oxford.

'Club Aegean was marvellous. I met my husband there!'
Meryl Irons, Los Angeles.

What do you have to do to go on holiday at Club Aegean?

* Fill in the coupon below and send it, with a 10% deposit, to Club Aegean, Inc. 276354 North Street East # 492, Bayou Canyon, Nevada.

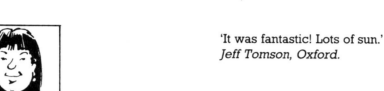

I would like to go to the Club Aegean from (*date*)

_____ to _____ 19_____

I enclose a 10% deposit. Please send me more details.

Name: _____

Address: _____

_____

_____

_____

Signed: _____ Date: _____

Schreiben Sie dann eine ähnliche Anzeige für

a) einen Kreuzfahrt-Dampfer (cruise ship),
b) eine Safari-Tour (wildlife safari),
c) eine Sprachenschule (language school).

Interaction

1 :::

1 Write a different word in each square below.
2 Divide into two teams.
3 A member from team **A** chooses a number from 1–16.
4 A member from team **B** says his word for that number.
5 The member from team **A** uses that word in a sentence or question and gets a point if he or she uses it correctly.

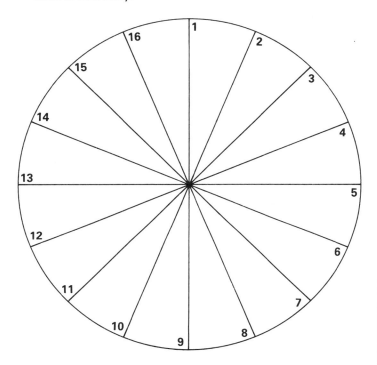

2 :

Student **A**: Look at number 10 on page 80. Complete the text with information that **B** has.
Student **B**: Look at number 10 on pages 86. Complete the text with information that **A** has.
Do not look at each other's texts until you have finished.

When was Elvis Presley born?

What was his wife's name?

Listening and acting out

1

Listen to the cassette and answer the questions.

1 Did Gerald like the exam?
2 Did Mick like the exam?
3 Did Gerald know Judy's name?
4 Is Gerald going to go to the party tonight?

2

Look at these questions from Gerald, Mick and Judy's exam. Listen to the cassette and then put the correct number for each question in the brackets.

ECONOMICS
Paper 2

Answer 3 questions.

(☐) Is the cost of medicine going to increase or decrease in the next twenty years?

(☐) What are the main uses of computers in the modern world?

(☐) The price of oil caused the world recession. Discuss.

(☐) What is the relationship between production and jobs in a recession?

(☐) Why is an increase in car production a problem?

3

You have just finished an exam. In small groups say if you liked the exam and arrange a party for tonight.

Language summary

Redewendungen

He fell off his bicycle, didn't he?	Er fiel vom Fahrrad, nicht?
He's a teacher, isn't he?	Er ist Lehrer, nicht wahr?
Why didn't Sylvie write postcards? – Because she read a book.	Warum hat Sylvie keine Postkarten geschrieben? Weil sie ein Buch gelesen hat.
We enjoyed having you.	Wir haben dich/Sie gern bei uns gehabt.
– I'll give you a call. We'll look forward to that. – Not at all.	Ich rufe Sie an. Darauf freuen wir uns. Aber das ist doch selbstverständlich.

Neue Wörter

production [prə'dʌkʃn]	Produktion
recession [rɪ'seʃn]	Wirtschaftsflaute
success [sək'ses]	Erfolg
learn [lɜːn]	lernen
social activities ['səuʃl æk'tɪvətɪz]	gemeinsame Unternehmungen
continue [kən'tɪnjuː]	fortsetzen
studies ['stʌdɪz]	Studien
grammar ['græmə]	Grammatik
textbook ['tekstbʊk]	Lehrbuch
month [mʌnθ]	Monat

Grammatik

Das Frageanhängsel (tag question)

They are Spanish, **aren't they?**	Das sind Spanier, nicht?
She lives in Cambridge, **doesn't she?**	Sie wohnt in Cambridge, nicht wahr?
They are going to start their honeymoon, **aren't they?**	Sie gehen jetzt in die Flitterwochen, oder?
She broke her leg, **didn't she?**	Sie hat sich ein Bein gebrochen, ja?

Das **Frageanhängsel** entspricht dem deutschen **nicht wahr?, nicht?, oder?, ja?**. Im Frageanhängsel wird das Hilfsverb des vorausgehenden Satzes wieder aufgenommen, und zwar verneint oder bejaht, umgekehrt zum vorausgehenden Satz. Ist kein Hilfsverb vorhanden, wird die entsprechende Form von *do* gewählt.

enjoy und *look forward to*

enjoy (= sich amüsieren, etwas genießen, sich über etwas freuen) kann sowohl für eine Handlung der Vergangenheit als auch für eine Handlung in der Zukunft gebraucht werden.
look forward to (= sich auf etwas freuen) kann nur im Zusammenhang mit einer zukünftigen Handlung gebraucht werden.

---

1 Redewendungen

Die folgenden Redewendungen sind durcheinander geraten.
Schreiben Sie auf, wie sie richtig zusammengehören.

I'll be *take an umbrella.*
I'll look forward *I'm late.*
You'd better *in touch.*
Thank you *talking to you.*
We enjoyed *for inviting me.*

How do you *some coffee.*
I'd rather *to that.*
I'm sorry *some help?*
Do you want *not.*
I'd prefer *take it?*

1 **I'll be in touch.**

2 ......

3 ......

4 ......

5 ......

6 ......

7 ......

8 ......

9 ......

10 ......

2 Frageanhängsel

Setzen Sie das richtige Frageanhängsel ein. Beispiel: You are Australian, *aren't you* ?

1 Jane cannot speak Portuguese, ...?

2 Sofia is a tourist guide, ...?

3 Jane Austen wrote novels, ...?

4 Tom is going to get married, ...?

5 Steve and Joan are not teaching right now, ...?

6 Paul does not like octopus, ...?

7 Sofia drove to Naples, ...?

8 Peter Smith does not live in Washington, ...?

9 You are going to get wet, ...?

10 Jane did not write her report, ...?

3 Zur Wiederholung

Entscheiden Sie sich für *a* oder *b*.

Beispiel: I **a** were / **b** was in London. ....*b*....

1 There **a** aren't / **b** isn't any cheese in the cupboard. ....

2 My mother · **a** she is / **b** is fifty-two years old. ....

3 Where **a** did you / **b** you did go yesterday? ....

4 I want to **a** swimming / **b** swim. ....

5 **a** Did you / **b** Do you see your friend yesterday? ....

4 Wortstellung

Ordnen Sie die Kästchen so, daß korrekte Sätze entstehen.
Setzen Sie Großbuchstaben, wo es nötig ist.

Beispiel: | in hong kong | yesterday | | i was |

I was in Hong Kong yesterday.

1 | at six o'clock | get up | . | every morning | has to | she |

....

2 | to the shops | but | peter | get wet | . | does not want to | has | to | he | go | . |

....

3 | a piano | ? | their house | peter and lucy | got | in | have |

....

4 | between | the hospital | the bank | is | . | and the station |

....

5 | caroline | every day | ? | what | at work | have to do | does |

....

5 Zur Wiederholung

Setzen Sie jeweils ein Wort in die Lücken des Dialogs.

SHEILA: Hey, Sheila! **1**............................. look worried! What's **2**............................. matter?

MELANIE: I can't find my keys and I have **3**............................. be at the folk club in **4**............................. an hour.

SHEILA: **5**............................. you going to meet someone there?

MELANIE: No, I'm **6**............................. to sing.

SHEILA: How often do you **7**............................. at the club?

MELANIE: This is only the **8**............................. time. I sang there **9**............................. week.

SHEILA: Was it a success?

MELANIE: Yes, I **10**............................. so. Look, you can't see my keys, can you?

SHEILA: What about those ones **11**............................. the table?

MELANIE: Oh, yes! Thanks. I have to go. I'll **12**............................. you on Thursday for lunch.

6 Lesen und schreiben Sie

Lesen Sie die folgenden Berichte, die Schüler(innen) einer Fremdsprachenschule am Ende des Semesters geschrieben haben.

I liked the English Course but it was very difficult for me. I wanted more grammar but the other students wanted more conversation, etc.

I think nearly all the teachers were good, but not mr Rushton. He can not teach.

I am going to return to this school again

I want to speak good English.

My English class was very good and it was often very interesting. We had a lot of grammar (I like grammar) and I liked the textbook.

The teachers were nice – especially Mr. Rushton. I think he is excellent – very well-prepared. (He is also very good-looking).

My English course was great fun. I think I learnt a lot. My teachers were very good.

We had to study a lot at home and I did not like that! I did not have much time for social activities.

I am going to continue my studies in Japan.

Schreiben Sie einen ähnlichen Bericht über Ihren eigenen Sprachkurs.

1

Fragen Sie: What does _____ do?   Where does _____ live?   Where is _____ now?
Ergänzen Sie das Formular.

NAME	John	Anne	Tim	Sue
HOME		Liverpool		New York
OCCUPATION	policeman			nurse
NOW		at home	at school	

2

Fragen Sie:
Where does/do _____ live?
Fragen Sie nach Ken, Jane, Mark und Rose,
Steve und Sue.
Setzen Sie ihre Namen an die richtige Stelle auf der Karte.

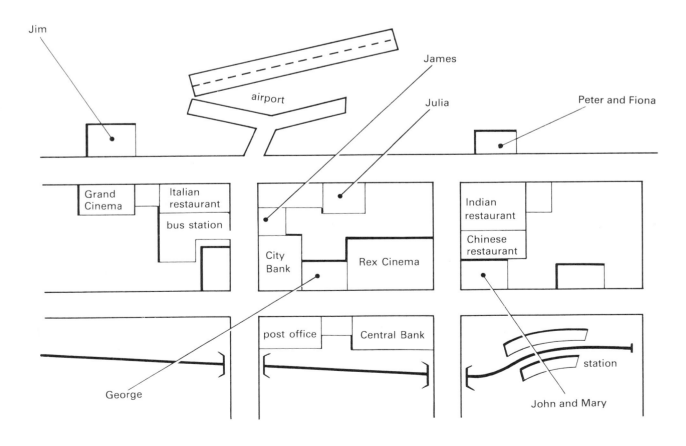

3

Fragen Sie: Where was/were _____ at _____ o'clock. Setzen Sie ihre Namen in die richtigen Zimmer ein.
Fragen Sie nach Peter, Katie, Mary und Laura.

20:30 hrs

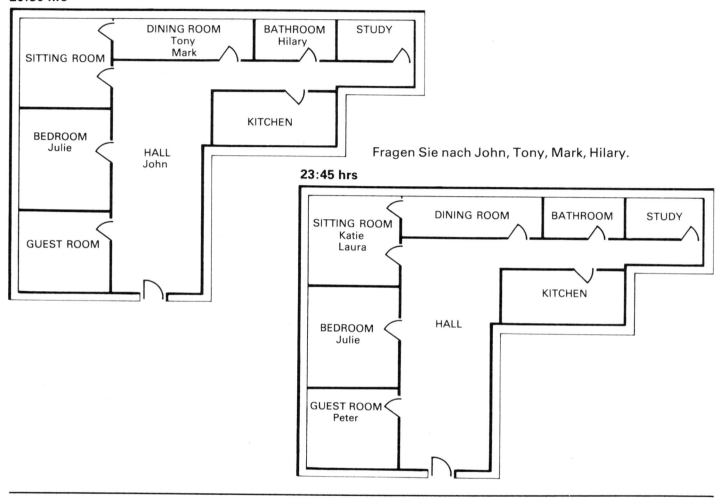

Fragen Sie nach John, Tony, Mark, Hilary.

23:45 hrs

4

Fragen Sie: Where does flight _____ _____?
What time does flight _____ _____?
Which gate?

FLIGHT NUMBER	DESTINATION	DEPARTURE	ARRIVAL (LT*)	GATE
389	Paris			6
560		1345		
027			1645	
951		1400		2
006			1630	
323	Tokyo			
*LT = local time				

5

1 Malen Sie die Schuhe, die Hose, den Pullover, die Augen und das Haar des Mannes farbig aus, oder schreiben Sie die Farben in die Zeichnung.

2 Finden Sie mindestens vier Gemeinsamkeiten mit dem Bild in Abschnitt B.

A

6

Fragen Sie: Does Tom like _____? Can Steve and Joan _____?

SPORT	Tom likes	ability	Steve and Joan like	ability
skiing				
skating	✓	✗	✗	✗
swimming				
boxing	✗	✗	✗	✗
(playing) golf				
(playing) baseball	✓	✗	✓	✗
(playing) tennis				
(playing) football	✓	✓	✗	✗

7

Fragen Sie: What does _____ do? How old is _____?
Is _____ _____ing now? How often does _____ _____?

Füllen Sie die Tabelle aus.

NAME	Keith	Pauline	Tony and Pat	Diana and Kate	Richard and Roger
OCCUPATION	painter		singers		teachers
AGE			Tony: 19 Pat: 21		Richard: 39 Roger: 42
RIGHT NOW	jogging		swimming		watching a video film
FREQUENCY OF ACTIVITY			four/five times a week		twice a week

8

Fragen Sie:

How much _____ is there?

How many _____ are there?

ITEM	AMOUNT	ITEM	AMOUNT
tea		onions	60 kilos
coffee	50 kilos	tomatoes	
sugar		potatoes	110 kilos
		mushrooms	
milk	80 litres	aubergines	35 kilos
butter		carrots	
cheese	26 kilos		
eggs			

9

ELVIS PRESLEY
☆ King of Rock and Roll ☆

In any book about pop music you will find the name Elvis Presley. And in many textbooks for students of English his story is told. Why? Why is Elvis Presley so famous?

Elvis Presley sang rock and roll. His record . . . . (made in 1956) sold one million copies. He starred in many films and was the idol of singers like the Beatles and the Rolling Stones.

Elvis Presley was born on . . . . His parents were Vernon Presley and Gladys Smith. They lived in . . . ., Mississippi. In January 1942 Elvis' father gave him a . . . . and the young boy started to play.

In . . . . the Presley family went to live in Memphis, Tennessee. After school Elvis worked as a . . . . In 1953 Elvis went to Sun Records. He paid . . . . and recorded a song for his mother. A girl from the record company heard the song and Elvis made a record for them called *That's all right Mama*. It was a great success and Elvis was soon very famous.

In . . . . Elvis joined the United States Army and went to Germany. There he met a young girl called . . . . They were married in the United States on 1st May, 1967. They had a daughter called . . . . But Elvis was always away from home — in Hollywood or Las Vegas — and Priscilla was unhappy. They got divorced.

Elvis Presley died on 16th August, ..., but people have still not forgotten him. He changed pop music for ever.

B

1

Fragen Sie: What does _____ do?   Where does _____ live?   Where is _____ now?
Füllen Sie das Formular aus.

NAME	John	Anne	Tim	Sue
HOME	London		San Francisco	
OCCUPATION		housewife	student	
NOW	at work			at work

2

Fragen Sie:
Where does/do _____ live?
Fragen Sie nach Julie, John und Mary,
George, Peter und Fiona, James.
Setzen Sie ihre Namen an die richtige Stelle auf der Karte.

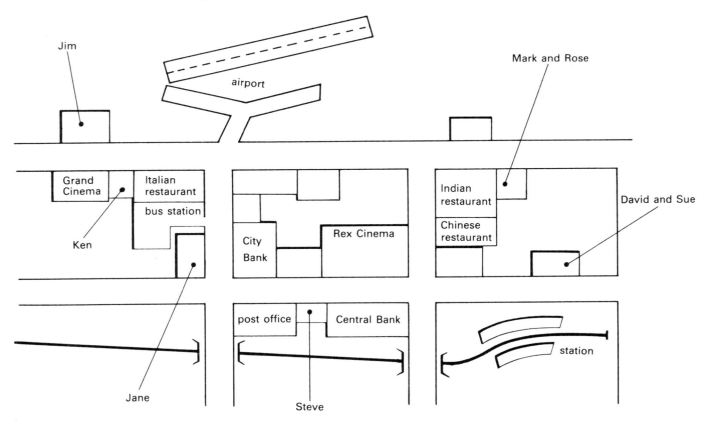

3

Fragen Sie: Where was/were _____ at _____ o'clock? Setzen Sie ihre Namen in die richtigen Zimmer ein.

Fragen Sie nach John, Hilary, Tony und Mark, Julie.

20:30 hrs

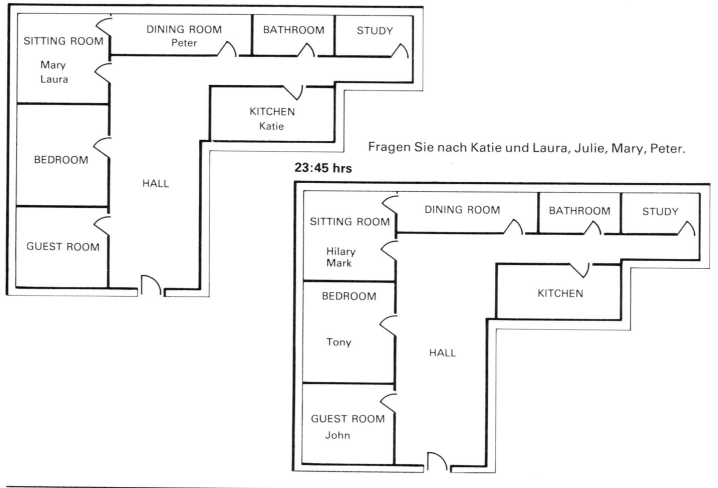

Fragen Sie nach Katie und Laura, Julie, Mary, Peter.

23:45 hrs

4

Fragen Sie: Where does flight _____ _____?
What time does flight _____ _____?
Which gate?

FLIGHT NUMBER	DESTINATION	DEPARTURE	ARRIVAL (LT*)	GATE
389		1330		
560	Madrid			9
027		1350		
951			2100	
006	Istanbul			
323		1425		13
*LT = local time				

B

5

1 Malen Sie die Schuhe, die Hose, den Pullover, die Augen und
  das Haar der Frau farbig aus, oder schreiben Sie die Farben in
  die Zeichnung.

2 Finden Sie mindestens vier Gemeinsamkeiten mit dem Bild in
  Abschnitt A.

6

Fragen Sie: Does Tom like _____?   Can Steve and Joan _____?

SPORT	Tom likes	ability	Steve and Joan like	ability
skiing	✓	✓	✗	✗
skating				
swimming	✓	✓	✓	✓
boxing				
(playing) golf	✓	✓	✗	✗
(playing) baseball				
(playing) tennis	✗	✗	✓	✗
(playing) football				

7

Fragen Sie: What does _____ do?   How old is _____?
Is _____ _____ing now?   How often does _____ _____?

Füllen Sie die Tabelle aus.

NAME	Keith	Pauline	Tony and Pat	Diana and Kate	Richard and Roger
OCCUPATION		actress		dancers	
AGE	69	26		Diana: 22 Kate: 31	
RIGHT NOW		having a bath		dancing	
FREQUENCY OF ACTIVITY	every day	twice a day		every morning and five nights a week	

B

8

Fragen Sie:
How much _____ is there?
How many _____ are there?

ITEM	AMOUNT	ITEM	AMOUNT
tea	48 kilos	onions	
coffee		tomatoes	35 kilos
sugar	120 kilos	potatoes	
		mushrooms	56 kilos
milk		aubergines	
butter	42 kilos	carrots	40 kilos
cheese			
eggs	500		

9

ELVIS PRESLEY
☆ King of Rock and Roll ☆

In any book about pop music you will find the name Elvis Presley. And in many textbooks for students of English his story is told. Why? Why is Elvis Presley so famous?

Elvis Presley sang rock and roll. His record *Heartbreak Hotel* (made in . . . .) sold one million copies. He starred in many films and was the idol of singers like the Beatles and the Rolling Stones.

Elvis Presley was born on 8th January, 1935. His parents were Vernon Presley and . . . . They lived in Tupelo, Mississippi. In . . . . Elvis' father gave him a guitar and the young boy started to play.

In 1948 the Presley family went to live in . . . ., Tennessee. After school Elvis worked as a lorry driver. In . . . . Elvis went to Sun Records. He paid $4 and recorded a song for his . . . . A girl from the record company heard the song and Elvis made a record for them called . . . . It was a great success and Elvis was soon very famous.

In 1958 Elvis joined the United States Army and went to . . . . There he met a young girl called Priscilla. They were married in the United States on . . . . They had a daughter called Lisa Marie. But Elvis was always away from home — in Hollywood or Las Vegas — and Priscilla was unhappy. They got divorced.

Elvis Presley died on . . . ., 1977, but people have still not forgotten him. He changed pop music for ever.

4

Fragen Sie: Where does flight _____   _____?
               What time does flight _____   _____?
               Which gate?

FLIGHT NUMBER	DESTINATION	DEPARTURE	ARRIVAL (LT*)	GATE
389			1420	
560			1425	
027	Lisbon			3
951	Mexico City			
006		1415		11
323			0825	
*LT = local time.				

9

Siehe Seite 47.

Siehe Seite 55.

Nationalitäten (zu Übung 1, Seite 11)

-an	-ish	-ese	irregular
Mexican	English	Japanese	French
Puerto Rican	Spanish	Portuguese	Swiss
German	Danish	Chinese	Greek
American	Swedish		Dutch
Australian	Turkish		
Brazilian	Irish		
Saudi Arabian			
Peruvian			
Hungarian			
Italian			
Argentinian			
Belgian			
Yugoslavian			

Wordlist

neues Wort	Übersetzung	unit
a [ə]	ein(e)	1
about [ə'baʊt]	über	1
actor ['æktə]	Schauspieler	1
am [æm]	bin	1
an [ən, æn]	ein(e)	1
and [ənd, ænd]	und	1
answer ['ɑ:nsə]	antworten	1
ask [ɑ:sk]	fragen	1
be [bi:]	sein	1
bus driver ['bʌs draɪvə]	Busfahrer(in)	1
businessman ['bɪznɪsmən]	Geschäftsmann	1
character ['kærəktə]	Person	1
conversation practice [ˌkɒnvə'seɪʃn 'præktɪs]	Gesprächsübung	1
crewman [krumæn]	Besatzungsmitglied	1
do [du]	tun (wird oft nicht übersetzt)	1
doctor ['dɒktə]	Arzt/Ärztin	1
down here [ˌdaʊn 'hɪə]	hier unten	1
driver ['draɪvə]	Fahrer	1
eight [eɪt]	acht	1
for [fɔ:]	für	1
hello [hə'ləʊ]	hallo	1
help! [help]	Hilfe!	1
home [həʊm]	Wohnort	1
housewife ['haʊswaɪf]	Hausfrau	1
I [aɪ]	ich	1
in [ɪn]	in	1
in the same way [ˌɪn ˌðə 'seɪm 'weɪ]	auf die gleiche Weise	1
is [ɪz]	ist	1
lawyer ['lɔ:jə]	Rechtsanwalt	1
like this [ˌlaɪk 'ðɪs]	wie hier	1
listen ['lɪsn]	zuhören	1
live [lɪv]	wohnen/leben	1
look [lʊk]	sehen	1
name [neɪm]	Name	1
nine [naɪn]	neun	1
nurse [nɜ:s]	Krankenschwester	1
occupation [ˌɒkjʊ'peɪʃn]	Beruf	1
oh [əʊ]	Null (beim Telefonieren)	1
one [wʌn]	eins	1
racing car mechanic ['reɪsɪŋ kɑ: mɪ'kænɪk]	Rennwagenmechaniker	1
racing driver ['reɪsɪŋ 'draɪvə]	Rennfahrer	1
read [ri:d]	lesen	1
say [seɪ]	sagen	1
secretary ['sekrətrɪ]	Sekretärin	1
seven ['sevn]	sieben	1
similar ['sɪmɪlə]	ähnlich	1
student ['stju:dnt]	Student	1
teacher ['ti:tʃə]	Lehrer	1
telephone ['telɪfəʊn]	Telefon	1
television reporter ['telɪˌvɪʒn rɪ'pɔ:tə]	Fernsehreporter(in)	1
the following numbers [ðə 'fɒləʊɪŋ 'nʌmbəz]	die folgenden Nummern	1
what [wʌt, wɒt]	was/wie	1
where [weə]	wo	1
write [raɪt]	schreiben	1
you [ju:]	du/Sie	1
your [jɔ:]	dein/Ihr	1
yours [jɔ:z]	deine(r)	1
are [ɑ:]	sind	2
at [ət, æt]	zu, an, bei	2
brother ['brʌðə]	Bruder	2
daughter ['dɔ:tə]	Tochter	2
does [dʌz]	sie tut (oft nicht übersetzt)	2
family tree ['fæməlɪ tri:]	Stammbaum	2
father ['fɑ:ðə]	Vater	2
Good afternoon [ˌgʊd ˌɑ:ftə'nu:n]	Guten Tag.	2
Goodbye [ˌgʊd'baɪ]	Auf Wiedersehen.	2
he [hi:]	er	2
husband ['hʌzbənd]	(Ehe-)mann	2
I think [aɪ θɪŋk]	Ich glaube	2
language focus ['læŋgwɪdʒ 'fəʊkəs]	Blickpunkt Sprache	2
madam ['mædəm]	Frau (als Anrede)	2
mother ['mʌðə]	Mutter	2
my [maɪ]	mein(e)	2
no [nəʊ]	nein	2
not [nɒt]	nicht	2
now [naʊ]	jetzt	2
please [pli:z]	bitte	2
school [sku:l]	Schule	2
she [ʃi:]	sie	2
sister ['sɪstə]	Schwester	2
son [sʌn]	Sohn	2
thank you ['θæŋk ju:]	danke	2
there [ðeə]	da	2
think [θɪŋk]	denken, meinen	2
wife [waɪf]	(Ehe-)frau	2
work [wɜ:k]	Arbeit	2
yes [jes]	ja	2
bank [bæŋk]	Bank, Geldinstitut	3
between [bɪ'twi:n]	zwischen	3
bus station ['bʌs ˌsteɪʃn]	Bushaltestelle	3
can [kæn]	kann	3
cinema ['sɪnəmə]	Kino	3
direction [dɪ'rekʃn]	Richtung	3
drama ['drɑ:mə]	Drama	3
excuse me! [ɪk'skju:z mi]	Entschuldigung!	3
glue [glu:]	Klebstoff	3
have [hæv]	haben	3
here [hɪə]	hier	3
here you are [hɪə ju: ɑ:]	bitte sehr (wenn man etwas gibt)	3
hey! [heɪ]	he!	3
house [haʊs]	Haus	3
I don't know [aɪ dəʊnt nəʊ]	Ich weiß es nicht.	3
I'm sorry [aɪm 'sɒrɪ]	es tut mir leid	3
it [ɪt]	es	3
man [mæn]	Mann	3
mention ['menʃn]	erwähnen	3
near [nɪə]	nahe	3
next to [nekstu:]	neben	3
of course [əv 'kɔ:s]	natürlich	3
on [ɒn]	auf	3
opposite ['ɒpəzɪt]	gegenüber	3
paragraph ['pærəgrɑ:f]	(Text-)Abschnitt	3
pen [pen]	Füllhalter	3
pencil ['pensl]	Bleistift	3
post office ['pəʊst ˌɒfɪs]	Postamt	3
remember [rɪ'membə]	denken Sie daran	3
restaurant ['restərɒŋ]	Gaststätte, Restaurant	3
road [rəʊd]	(Land-)Straße	3
ruler [ru:lə]	Lineal	3
scissors ['sɪzəz]	Schere	
sellotape ['seləʊteɪp]	Tesafilm	3
shelf [ʃelf]	Regal	3
station ['steɪʃn]	Bahnhof	3
street [stri:t]	Straße	3
table [teɪbl]	Tisch	3
thanks [θæŋks]	dankeschön	3
the [ðə]	der/die/das	3
theatre ['θɪətə]	Theater	3
their [ðeə]	ihr(e)	3
woman ['wʊmən]	Frau	3
age [eɪdʒ]	Alter	4
Australia [ɒ'streɪljə]	Australien	4
Australian [ɒ'streɪljən]	Australier(in)	4
box [bɒks]	Kasten	4
British ['brɪtɪʃ]	britisch/Brite/Britin	4
but [bʌt]	aber	4
chart [tʃɑ:t]	Karte, Diagramm	4
choose [tʃu:z]	wählen	4
correct [kə'rekt]	richtig	4
France [frɑ:ns]	Frankreich	4
French [frentʃ]	französisch/Franzose/ Französin	4
from [frəm]	aus, von	4
German ['dʒɜ:mən]	deutsch/Deutscher/ Deutsche	4
Germany ['dʒɜ:mənɪ]	Deutschland	
Greece [gri:s]	Griechenland	4
Greek [gri:k]	griechisch/Grieche/Griechin	4
Italian [ɪ'tæljən]	italienisch/Italiener(in)	4
Italy ['ɪtəlɪ]	Italien	4
Japanese [ˌdʒæpə'ni:z]	japanisch/Japaner(in)	4
meet [mi:t]	treffen	4
Mexican ['meksɪkən]	mexikanisch/Mexikaner(in)	4
Mexico ['meksɪkəʊ]	Mexiko	4
nationality [ˌnæʃə'næləti]	Nationalität	4
Pleased to meet you ['pli:zd tə mi:t ju:]	Nett, Sie zu treffen.	4
Portuguese ['pɔ:tjʊ'gi:z]	portugiesisch/Portugiese(in)	4

neues Wort	Übersetzung	unit
repeat [rɪ'pi:t]	wiederholen	4
secret ['si:krɪt]	Geheimnis	4
Spain [speɪn]	Spanien	4
Spanish ['spænɪʃ]	spanisch/Spanier(in)	4
that [ðət]	das	4
this [ðɪs]	dieser, diese, dieses	4
to [tə, tu:]	zu, in	4
we [wi:]	wir	4
welcome ['welkəm]	willkommen	4
afternoon [,ɑ:ftə'nu:n]	Nachmittag	5
alone [ə'ləʊn]	allein	5
back [bæk]	zurück	5
come in [kʌm ɪn]	komm rein	5
evening ['i:vnɪŋ]	Abend	5
forgot [fə'gɒt]	vergaß	5
Friday ['fraɪdi]	Freitag	5
hospital ['hɒspɪtl]	Krankenhaus	5
hotel [həʊ'tel]	Hotel	5
Monday ['mʌndi]	Montag	5
morning ['mɔ:nɪŋ]	Morgen	5
on Monday [ɒn 'mʌndi]	am Montag	5
Saturday ['sætədi]	Samstag	5
speaking ['spi:kɪŋ]	spricht gerade	5
Sunday ['sʌndi]	Sonntag	5
supermarket ['su:pə,mɑ:kɪt]	Supermarkt	5
then [ðen]	dann	5
these [ði:z]	diese	5
three o'clock [ðri: ə'klɒk]	drei Uhr	5
Thursday ['θɜ:zdi]	Donnerstag	5
time [taɪm]	Zeit	5
tour guide ['tʊə gaɪd]	Reiseleiter(in)	5
Tuesday ['tju:zdi]	Dienstag	5
was [wəz, wɒz]	war	5
Wednesday ['wenzdeɪ]	Mittwoch	5
were [wɜ:]	waren	5
who [hu:]	wer	5
with [wɪð]	mit	5
yesterday ['jestədi]	gestern	5
again [ə'gen]	wieder	6
attendant [ə'tendənt]	Aufsichtsbeamter	6
book [bʊk]	Buch	6
boots [bu:ts]	Stiefel	6
borrow ['bɒrəʊ]	von jemdm. leihen	6
boyfriend ['bɔɪfrend]	Freund	6
Brazilian [brə'zɪljən]	Brasilianer(in)	6
camera ['kæmərə]	Kamera	6
cameraman ['kæmərəmən]	Kameramann	6
Canadian [kə'neɪdjən]	Kanadier(in)	6
come [kʌm]	kommen	6
equipment [ɪ'kwɪpmənt]	Ausrüstung	6
everybody ['evrɪbɒdi]	jeder	6
glasses [glɑ:sɪz]	Brille	6
gloves [glʌvz]	Handschuhe	6
here we go! ['hɪə wi: gəʊ]	Es geht los!	6
hers [hɜ:z]	ihr(e/es)	6
his [hɪz]	sein(e/r/s)	6
jacket ['dʒækɪt]	Jacke	6
lighter ['laɪtə]	Feuerzeug	6
matches ['mætʃɪz]	Streichhölzer	6
mine [maɪn]	mein(e/er)	6
ours ['aʊəz]	unser(e/es)	6
parents ['peərənts]	Eltern	6
passenger ['pæsɪndʒə]	passagier	6
present ['prezənt]	gegenwärtig	6
shirt [ʃɜ:t]	Oberhemd	6
shoes [ʃu:z]	Schuhe	6
sir [sɜ:]	mein Herr	6
skirt [skɜ:t]	Rock	6
sweater [swetə]	Pullover	6
theirs [ðeəz]	ihr(e/es) (Mehrzahl)	6
they [ðeɪ]	sie (Mehrzahl)	6
this way [ðɪs weɪ]	hier entlang	6
those [ðəʊz]	diese da	6
today [tə'deɪ]	heute	6
tomorrow [tə'mɒrəʊ]	morgen	6
trousers ['traʊzəz]	Hosen	6
way [weɪ]	Weg	6
whose [hu:z]	wessen	6
word [wɜ:d]	Wort	6
address [ə'dres]	Anschrift	7
advertisement [əd'vɜ:tɪsmənt]	Anzeige, Inserat	7
ago [ə'gəʊ]	vor	7

neues Wort	Übersetzung	unit
airline ['eəlaɪn]	Fluggesellschaft	7
all [ɔ:l]	alle	7
all right [ɔ:l 'raɪt]	in Ordnung	7
America [ə'merɪkə]	Amerika	7
another [ə'nʌðə]	ein(e) andere(r)	7
appointment [ə'pɔɪntmənt]	Verabredung	7
below [bɪ'ləʊ]	unten	7
big [bɪg]	groß	7
birthday ['bɜ:θdeɪ]	Geburtstag	7
book [bʊk]	buchen	7
car [kɑ:]	Auto	7
certainly ['sɜ:tnli]	sicherlich	7
clock face ['klɒk feɪs]	Zifferblatt	7
colleague ['kɒli:g]	Kollege	7
complete [kəm'pli:t]	vervollständigen	7
copy ['kɒpi]	abschreiben	7
daily ['deɪli]	täglich	7
date [deɪt]	Datum	7
day [deɪ]	Tag	7
exciting [ɪk'saɪtɪŋ]	aufregend	7
flight [flaɪt]	Flug	7
fly [flaɪ]	fliegen	7
girlfriend ['gɜ:lfrend]	Freundin	7
Good morning [,gʊd'mɔ:nɪŋ]	Guten Morgen.	7
hairdresser's ['heə,dresəz]	Friseur(geschäft)	7
happy ['hæpi]	glücklich	7
harbour ['hɑ:bə]	Hafen	7
hire ['haɪə]	mieten	7
job [dʒɒb]	Beruf	7
last [lɑ:st]	letzte(r/s)	7
life [laɪf]	Leben	7
make [meɪk]	machen	7
newest ['nju:ɪst]	neueste(r/s)	7
newspaper ['nju:s,peɪpə]	Zeitung	7
next [nekst]	nächste(r/s)	7
opera house ['ɒpərəhaʊs]	Opernhaus	7
past [pɑ:st]	nach	7
people [pi:pl]	Leute	7
place [pleɪs]	Ort	7
problem ['prɒbləm]	Problem	7
race [reɪs]	Rennen	7
read [red]	las	7
reason [ri:zn]	Grund	7
revision [rɪ'vɪʒn]	Wiederholung	7
room [ru:m]	Zimmer	7
sentence ['sentəns]	Satz	7
tonight [tə'naɪt]	heute Abend/Nacht	7
tower ['taʊə]	Turm	7
travel ['trævl]	reisen	7
use [ju:z]	gebrauchen	7
waiter ['weɪtə]	Kellner	7
want [wɒnt]	wollen, mögen	7
when [wen]	wann	7
will [wɪl]	wird	7
world [wɜ:ld]	Welt	7
acting class ['æktɪŋ,klɑ:s]	Schauspielunterricht	8
answer ['ɑ:nsə]	Antwort	8
best [best]	am besten	8
boxing ['bɒksɪŋ]	Boxen	8
bullfighting ['bʊlfaɪtɪŋ]	Stierkampf	8
cheese [tʃi:z]	Käse	8
chilli ['tʃɪli]	Pfefferschote	8
chocolate ['tʃɒkələt]	Schokolade	8
city ['sɪti]	(Innen-)Stadt	8
classmate ['klɑ:smeɪt]	Klassenkamerad(in)	8
could [kʊd]	könnte(n/st)	8
country ['kʌntri]	Land	8
courgette [,kʊə'ʒet]	Zucchini	8
dish [dɪʃ]	Tellergericht	8
end [end]	Ende	8
English ['ɪŋglɪʃ]	englisch	8
famous ['feɪməs]	berühmt	8
fast [fɑ:st]	schnell	8
favourite ['feɪvərɪt]	Lieblings-	8
fish [fɪʃ]	Fisch	8
food [fu:d]	Speise(n)	8
football ['fʊtbɔ:l]	Fußball	8
go [gəʊ]	gehen	8
good [gʊd]	gut	8
hate [heɪt]	hassen	8
library ['laɪbrəri]	Bücherei	8
like [laɪk]	mögen	8
look! [lʊk]	sehen Sie!	8

neues Wort	Übersetzung	unit	neues Wort	Übersetzung	unit
love [lʌv]	lieben	8	price [praɪs]	Preis	9
lunch [lʌntʃ]	Mittagessen	8	quite [kwaɪt]	ziemlich	9
match [mætʃ]	verbinden	8	recognise ['rekəgnaɪz]	erkennen	9
minced meat ['mɪnstmiːt]	Hackfleisch	8	return ticket [rɪ'tɜːn 'tɪkɪt]	Rückfahrkarte	9
must [mʌst]	muß	8	single ['sɪŋgl]	Einzelfahrschein	9
neighbour ['neɪbə]	Nachbar(in)	8	success [sək'ses]	Erfolg	9
never ['nevə]	niemals	8	tall [tɔːl]	groß (von Gestalt)	9
octopus ['ɒktəpəs]	Tintenfisch	8	tell [tel]	erzählen	9
often ['ɒfn]	oft	8	ticket ['tɪkɪt]	(Fahr-)Karte	9
onions ['ʌnjənz]	Zwiebeln	8	train [treɪn]	Zug	9
our ['aʊə]	unser(e)	8	wake up [ˌweɪk'ʌp]	aufwachen	9
picture ['pɪktʃə]	Bild	8	watch [wɒtʃ]	(zu-)sehen	9
potatoes [pə'teɪtəʊz]	Kartoffeln	8	weekend [ˌwiː'k'end]	Wochenende	9
question ['kwestʃən]	Frage	8	went [went]	ging	9
raw [rɔː]	roh	8	which [wɪtʃ]	welche(r/s)	9
really ['rɪəli]	wirklich	8	airport ['eəpɔːt]	Flughafen	10
running ['rʌnɪŋ]	Laufen	8	article ['ɑːtɪkl]	Artikel	10
sauce [sɔːs]	Soße	8	blond [blɒnd]	blond	10
saw [sɔː]	sah(en)	8	blue [bluː]	blau	10
see [siː]	sehen	8	boy [bɔɪ]	Junge	10
singer ['sɪŋə]	Sänger	8	check in [ˌtʃek'ɪn]	sich anmelden	10
skiing ['skiːɪŋ]	Schilaufen	8	coffee ['kɒfi]	Kaffee	10
some (sʌm]	etwas	8	colour ['kʌlə]	Farbe	10
someone ['sʌmwʌn]	jemand	8	consume [kən'sjuːm]	verzehren	10
sport [spɔːt]	Sport	8	crowded ['kraʊdɪd]	überfüllt	10
study ['stʌdi]	studieren	8	describe [dɪ'skraɪb]	beschreiben	10
sun [sʌn]	Sonne	8	dog [dɒg]	Hund	10
survey ['sɜːveɪ]	Umfrage	8	earrings ['ɪərɪŋs]	Ohrringe	10
swimming ['swɪmɪŋ]	Schwimmen	8	employed [em'plɔɪd]	angestellt	10
talk [tɔːk]	sprechen	8	entrance ['entrəns]	Eingang	10
Taurus ['tɔːrəs]	Stier (Sternzeichen)	8	even ['iːvn]	selbst, sogar	10
tomato [tə'mɑːtəʊ]	Tomate	8	eyes [aɪz]	Augen	10
tried [traɪd]	versucht	8	facts [fækts]	Tatsachen	10
ugh! [ʊːx]	igitt!	8	family [fæməli]	Familie	10
until [ən'tɪl]	bis	8	fat [fæt]	dick, fett	10
usually ['juːʒʊəli]	gewöhnlich	8	figures [fɪgəz]	Zahlen	10
wait [weɪt]	warten	8	girl [gɜːl]	Mädchen	10
week [wiːk]	Woche	8	good-looking [ˌgʊd'lʊkɪŋ]	gut aussehend	10
well ... [wel]	also ...	8	green [griːn]	grün	10
air hostess ['eəˌhəʊstɪs]	Stewardess	9	grey [greɪ]	grau	10
arrive [ə'raɪv]	ankommen	9	hair [heə]	Haar	10
beard [bɪəd]	Bart	9	height [haɪt]	(Körper)größe	10
bed [bed]	Bett	9	help [help]	helfen	10
behind [bɪ'haɪnd]	hinter	9	horrible ['hɒrəbl]	schrecklich	10
bike [baɪk]	Fahrrad	9	ill [ɪl]	krank	10
black [blæk]	schwarz	9	large [lɑːdʒ]	groß	10
breakfast ['brekfəst]	Frühstück	9	look like ['lʊk laɪk]	aussehen	10
brown [braʊn]	braun	9	lost [lɒst]	verloren (gegangen)	10
by train [baɪ'treɪn]	mit dem Zug	9	medium ['miːdjəm]	mittelgroß	10
canteen [kæn'tiːn]	Kantine	9	middle-aged [ˌmɪdl'eɪdʒd]	mittleren Alters	10
chess [tʃes]	Schach	9	missing ['mɪsɪŋ]	vermißt	10
chief mechanic ['tʃiːf mɪ'kænɪk]	Chefmechaniker	9	nervous ['nɜːvəs]	nervös	10
			new [njuː]	neu	10
children ['tʃɪldrən]	Kinder	9	noisy ['nɔɪzi]	laut	10
darts [dɑːts]	engl. Pfeilspiel	9	of interest [əv 'ɪntrəst]	von Interesse, interessant	10
depart [dɪ'pɑːt]	abfahren	9	officer ['ɒfɪsə]	Herr Schutzmann (Anrede)	10
destination [ˌdestɪ'neɪʃn]	Endstation	9	old [əʊld]	alt	10
died [daɪd]	starb	9	one of ['wʌnˌəv]	ein(e/r) von	10
easily ['iːzɪli]	leicht	9	pair of ['peəˌəv]	ein Paar	10
exercise ['eksəsaɪz]	Sport	9	pint [paɪnt]	ca. 1/2 Liter	10
fair [feə]	blond	9	port [pɔːt]	Hafen	10
female ['fiːmeɪl]	weiblich	9	probably ['prɒbəbli]	wahrscheinlich	10
few [fjuː]	wenig(e)	9	programme ['prəʊgræm]	Programm	10
get home [get'həʊm]	nach Hause kommen	9	sandwich ['sænwɪdʒ]	belegtes Brot	10
get up [ˌget'ʌp]	aufstehen	9	short [ʃɔːt]	klein, kurz	10
go to bed [ˌgəʊ tə 'bed]	zu Bett gehen	9	size [saɪz]	Größe	10
how much [ˌhaʊ'mʌtʃ]	wie viel	9	small [smɔːl]	klein	10
Indian ['ɪndjən]	indisch	9	special [speʃl]	besonders	10
institute ['ɪnstɪtjuːt]	Institut	9	spot [spɒt]	Fleck	10
jogging ['dʒɒgɪŋ]	Dauerlauf	9	tea [tiː]	Tee	10
leave [liːv]	abfahren, verlassen	9	terminal ['tɜːmɪnl]	Schalter (Flughafen)	10
long [lɒŋ]	lang	9	thin [θɪn]	dünn	10
minute ['mɪnɪt]	Minute	9	tie [taɪ]	Krawatte	10
music ['mjuːzɪk]	Musik	9	typical ['tɪpɪkl]	typisch	10
north [nɔːθ]	im Norden	9	white [waɪt]	weiß	10
number ['nʌmbə]	Nummer	9	young [jʌŋ]	jung	10
on foot [ɒn 'fʊt]	zu Fuß	9	a little [ə'lɪtl]	ein bißchen	11
open ['əʊpən]	öffnen	9	ability [ə'bɪləti]	Fähigkeit	11
platform ['plætfɔːm]	Bahnsteig	9	American [ə'merɪkən]	amerikanisch/ Amerikaner(in)	11
play [pleɪ]	spielen	9			
plump [plʌmp]	vollschlank	9	buy [baɪ]	kaufen	11
policeman [pə'liːsmən]	Polizist	9	classical ['klæsɪkl]	klassisch	11
pound [paʊnd]	Pfund (Sterling)	9	clothes [kləʊðz]	Kleidung(sstücke)	11

neues Wort	Übersetzung	unit
concert ['kɒnsət]	Konzert	11
cook [kʊk]	kochen/Koch	11
disappear [ˌdɪsə'pɪə]	verschwinden	11
dress [dres]	Kleid	11
drive [draɪv]	fahren	11
early ['ɜ:li]	früh	11
Europe ['jʊərəp]	Europa	11
every ['evri]	jede(r/s)	11
exhausted [ɪg'zɔ:stɪd]	erschöpft	11
exhibition [ˌeksɪ'bɪʃn]	Ausstellung	11
film [fɪlm]	Film	11
find [faɪnd]	finden	11
gallery ['gælərɪ]	Galerie	11
garden ['gɑ:dn]	Garten	11
guitar [gɪ'tɑ:]	Gitarre	11
hall [hɔ:l]	Saal	11
hear [hɪə]	hören	11
homework ['ĥəʊmwɜ:k]	Hausaufgaben	11
idea [aɪ'dɪə]	Idee	11
interesting ['ɪntrɪstɪŋ]	interessant	11
island ['aɪlənd]	Insel	11
keys [ki:z]	Schlüssel	11
late [leɪt]	spät	11
Latin America	Lateinamerika	11
['lætɪn ə'merɪka]		
lift [lɪft]	aufheben	11
lines [laɪnz]	Zeilen, Text	11
night [naɪt]	Nacht	11
nobody ['nəʊbədɪ]	niemand	11
own [əʊn]	eigen(e/r/s)	11
painting ['peɪntɪŋ]	Gemälde	11
piano [pɪ'ænəʊ]	Klavier	11
Puerto Rican	Puertorikaner(in)	11
[ˌpwɜ:təʊ 'ri:kən]		
remember [rɪ'membə]	sich erinnern	11
royal ['rɔɪəl]	königlich	11
season [si:zn]	Saison, Serie	11
seat [si:t]	(Sitz-)Platz	11
shop [ʃɒp]	Geschäft	11
sit down [ˌsɪt 'daʊn]	sich setzen	11
skate [skeɪt]	Schlittschuh laufen	11
ski [ski:]	Schi laufen	11
sound [saʊnd]	klingen	11
speak [spi:k]	sprechen	11
start [stɑ:t]	starten	11
swimming pool	Schwimmbecken	11
['swɪmɪŋ pu:l]		
taken ['teɪkn]	besetzt	11
tired ['taɪəd]	müde	11
track [træk]	Rennbahn	11
try [traɪ]	versuchen	11
type [taɪp]	maschineschreiben	11
upset [ʌp'set]	aufgeregt	11
visit [vɪsɪt]	besuchen	11
worried ['wʌrɪd]	sorgenvoll	11
across [ə'krɒs]	über	12
always ['ɔ:lweɪz]	immer	12
Atlantic [ət'læntɪk]	Atlantik	12
badly [bædlɪ]	schlecht	12
be off [bɪ ɒf]	losgehen	12
beautiful ['bju:təfʊl]	schön	12
Canada ['kænədə]	Kanada	12
change [tʃeɪndʒ]	verändern	12
chess set ['tʃesset]	Schachspiel	12
coffee bar [kɒfi bɑ:]	Cafeteria	12
cover ['kʌvə]	Umschlag	12
crown [kraʊn]	Krone	12
dance [dɑ:ns]	Tanz(veranstaltung)	12
dear [dɪə]	liebe(r)	12
Endgame ['endgeɪm]	Endspiel	12
fantastic [fæn'tæstɪk]	phantastisch	12
flat [flæt]	Wohnung	12
give [gɪv]	geben	12
give me a game [gɪv mɪ ə	spiel mit mir	12
'geɪm]		
go out [gəʊ 'aʊt]	ausgehen	12
how often ['haʊ'ɒfən]	wie oft	12
how old]haʊ'əʊld]	wie alt	12
I'd = I would [aɪd]	ich möchte/würde	12
if [ɪf]	wenn, falls	12
jewel ['dʒu:əl]	Juwel	12
know [nəʊ]	wissen	12
let's [lets]	laß(t) uns	12
me [mi:]	mir/mich	12
meal [mi:l]	Mahlzeit	12
nothing ['nʌθɪŋ]	nichts	12
once [wʌns]	einmal	12
order ['ɔ:də]	Reihenfolge	12
ordinary ['ɔ:dnri]	gewöhnlich	12
paint [peɪnt]	malen	12
paints [peɪnts]	Farben	12
play [pleɪ]	Theaterstück	12
present ['prezənt]	Geschenk	12
quarrel ['kwɒrəl]	Streit	12
rarely ['reəli]	selten	12
record ['rekɔ:d]	Schallplatte	12
route [ru:t]	Route	12
row [raʊ]	Streit	12
sing [sɪŋ]	singen	12
sit [sɪt]	sitzen	12
skates [skeɪts]	Schlittschuhe	12
sleep [sli:p]	schlafen	12
sometimes ['sʌmtaɪmz]	manchmal	12
song [sɒŋ]	Lied	12
soon [su:n]	bald	12
speech [spi:tʃ]	Sprache, Rede	12
stay [steɪ]	wohnen	12
teach [ti:tʃ]	lehren	12
tennis racket ['tenɪs ˌrækɪt]	Tennisschläger	12
three times [ˌθri : 'taɪmz]	dreimal	12
too [tu:]	auch	12
true [tru:]	wahr	12
trumpet ['trʌmpɪt]	Trompete	12
tune [tju:n]	Melodie	12
twice [twaɪs]	zweimal	12
very [veri]	sehr	12
want to ['wɒntʊ]	wollen	12
well [wel]	gut	12
wrong [rɒŋ]	falsch, verkehrt	12
year [jɪə]	Jahr	12
ache [eɪk]	schmerzen	13
Alps [ælps]	Alpen	13
anyway ['enɪweɪ]	jedenfalls	13
beach [bi:tʃ]	Strand	13
briefcase [bri:fkeɪs]	Aktentasche	13
car park ['kɑ:pɑ:k]	Parkhaus	13
Caribbean [kærɪ'bi:ən]	Karibik	13
chop [tʃɒp]	(klein-)schneiden	13
Christmas ['krɪsməs]	Weihnachten	13
climb [klaɪm]	klettern	13
cool [ku:l]	kühl	13
delicious [dɪ'lɪʃəs]	köstlich	13
dentist ['dentɪst]	Zahnarzt	13
drink [drɪnk]	Getränk	13
egg [eg]	Ei	13
electrician [ˌɪlek'trɪʃn]	Elektriker	13
envelope ['envələʊp]	Briefumschlag	13
feel [fi:l]	fühlen	13
file [faɪl]	Akte	13
floor [flɔ:]	Fußboden	13
fry [fraɪ]	braten	13
garage ['gærɑ:ʒ]	Werkstatt, Garage	13
hitchhike ['hɪtʃhaɪk]	per Anhalter fahren	13
holiday ['hɒlədi]	Urlaub, Ferien	13
hurt [hɜ:t]	schmerzen	13
I'd rather not [ˌaɪd 'rɑ:ðə ˌnɒt]	ich möchte lieber nicht	13
ingredients [ɪn'gri:dɪənts]	Zutaten	13
jeweller ['dʒu:ələ]	Juwelier	13
just [dʒʌst]	gerade (jetzt)	13
knee [ni:]	Knie	13
lie [laɪ]	liegen	13
limp [lɪmp]	humpeln	13
lovely ['lʌvli]	herrlich	13
money [mʌni]	Geld	13
moustache [mə'stɑ:ʃ]	Schnurrbart	13
oh dear! [əʊ 'dɪə]	ach du meine Güte!	13
omelette [ɒmlet]	Omelett	13
painter ['peɪntə]	Maler	13
pan [pæn]	Pfanne	13
peel [pi:l]	schälen	13
pepper ['pepə]	Pfeffer	13
perhaps [pə'hæps]	vielleicht	13
pick [pɪk]	aufsammeln	13
plate [pleɪt]	Teller	13
postcard ['pəʊstkɑ:d]	Postkarte	13
put [pʊt]	hineintun	13

neues Wort	Übersetzung	unit
ready [redi]	fertig	13
recipe ['resɪpi]	Rezept	13
rest [rest]	sich ausruhen	13
right now [ˌraɪt 'naʊ]	gerade jetzt	13
sail [seɪl]	segeln	13
slow [sləʊ]	langsam	13
smell [smel]	riechen, duften	13
suppose [sə'pəʊz]	vermuten	13
surveillance [sɜː'veɪləns]	Überwachung	13
take [teɪk]	bringen, nehmen	13
taste [teɪst]	probieren, kosten	13
terrible ['terəbl]	schrecklich	13
tooth [tuːθ]	Zahn	13
town [taʊn]	Stadt	13
transcript ['trænskrɪpt]	Abschrift	13
umbrella [ʌm'brelə]	Regenschirm	13
vegetable ['vedʒtəbl]	Gemüse	13
vet [vet]	Tierarzt	13
wash [wɒʃ]	waschen	13
watch [wɒtʃ]	Armbanduhr	13
what's the matter? [wɒts ðə 'mætə]	was ist los?	13
why [waɪ]	warum	13
work [wɜːk]	arbeiten	13
after ['ɑːftə]	nach	14
any [enɪ]	irgendwelche	14
area ['eɪrɪə]	Gebiet	14
bag [bæg]	Tasche	14
ballpoint (pen) ['bɒlpɔɪnt] [pen]	Kugelschreiber	14
bookshop ['bʊkʃɒp]	Buchladen	14
both [bəʊθ]	beide	14
branch [brɑːntʃ]	Filiale	14
butter ['bʌtə]	Butter	14
capital city ['kæpɪtl'sɪtɪ]	Hauptstadt	14
cigarette [sɪgə'ret]	Zigarette	14
citizen ['sɪtɪzn]	Staatsbürger	14
correcting fluid [kə'rektɪŋ fluːɪd]	Tippex	14
Danish [deɪnɪʃ]	dänisch	14
dependency [dɪ'pendənsi]	abhängiges Gebiet	14
descent [dɪsent]	Abstammung	14
Dutch [dʌtʃ]	holländisch	14
ending [endɪŋ]	enden	14
eraser [ɪ'reɪzə]	Radiergummi	14
felt-tip (pen) [feltɪp] [pen]	Filzstift	14
goods [gʊdz]	Waren	14
gun [gʌn]	Pistole	14
have you got? [hævjʊ'gɒt]	haben Sie?	14
however [hʊ'evə]	jedoch	14
in stock [in'stɒk]	auf Lager	14
independence [ˌɪndɪ'pendəns]	Unabhängigkeit	14
industry ['ɪndəstri]	Industrie	14
Irish ['aɪərɪʃ]	irisch	14
item ['aɪtəm]	(Handels-)Artikel	14
Kenyan ['Kenjən]	aus Kenia	14
kind (of) [kaɪnd]	Sorte	14
lion ['laɪən]	Löwe	14
magazine [ˌmægə'ziːn]	Zeitschrift	14
map [mæp]	Karte	14
milk [mɪlk]	Milch	14
mistake [mɪ'steɪk]	Fehler	14
newsagent ['njuːzˌeɪdʒənt]	Zeitschriftenhändler	14
no longer [nəʊ 'lɒŋgə]	nicht länger	14
only ['əʊnli]	nur	14
paper clip ['peɪpəklɪp]	Büroklammer	14
passport ['pɑːspɔːt]	Reisepaß	14
per cent [pə'sent]	Prozent	14
petrochemical plant [petrəʊ'kemɪkl plɑːnt]	petrochemische Fabrik	14
pharmaceutical [ˌfɑːmə'sjuːtɪkl]	pharmazeutisch	14
photograph ['fəʊtəgrɑːf]	Foto	14
pocket ['pɒkɪt]	Tasche	14
population [ˌpɒpjʊ'leɪʃn]	Bevölkerung	14
prefer [prɪ'fɜː]	vorziehen	14
report [rɪ'pɔːt]	Bericht	14
sell [sel]	verkaufen	14
silly [sɪli]	dumm	14
situated ['sɪtjʊeɪtɪd]	gelegen	14
south [saʊθ]	Süden	14
staple [steɪpl]	Heftklammer	14
statement ['steɪtmənt]	Aussage	14
stationery ['steɪʃnəri]	Briefpapier	14
stock [stɒk]	Lager	14
store [stɔː]	Laden	14
sugar ['ʃʊgə]	Zucker(würfel)	14
Swiss [swɪs]	schweizerisch	14
thousand ['θaʊzənd]	tausend	14
tiger ['taɪgə]	Tiger	14
torch [tɔːtʃ]	Taschenlampe	14
without [wɪ'ðaʊt]	ohne	14
a lot [ə'lɒt]	eine Menge	15
accident ['æksɪdənt]	Unfall	15
agriculture ['ægrɪˌkʌltʃə]	Landwirtschaft	15
bridge [brɪdʒ]	Brücke	15
bruise [bruːz]	Schramme	15
cash [kæʃ]	Bargeld	15
cat [kæt]	Katze	15
cheque [tʃek]	Scheck	15
chicken ['tʃɪkɪn]	Hähnchen	15
clean [kliːn]	reinigen	15
cliff [klɪf]	Steilküste	15
coal [kəʊl]	Kohle	15
credit card ['kredɪtkɑːd]	Kreditkarte	15
crew [kruː]	Mannschaft	15
cut [kʌt]	Schnittverletzung	15
detail ['diːteɪl]	Einzelheit	15
dramatic [drə'mætɪk]	dramatisch	15
entertainment [ˌentə'teɪnmənt]	Unterhaltung(sangebot)	15
factory ['fæktri]	Fabrik	15
fine [faɪn]	gut, fein	15
Gosh! [gɒʃ]	Erstaunlich!	15
heavy traffic [ˌhevɪ'træfɪk]	dichter Verkehr	15
how many [haʊ 'menɪ]	wie viele	15
information [ˌɪnfə'meɪʃn]	Information	15
injury ['ɪndʒəri]	Verletzung	15
lake [leɪk]	See	15
litre ['liːtə]	Liter	15
many ['menɪ]	viele	15
market [mɑːkɪt]	Markt	15
mountain ['maʊntɪn]	Berg	15
much [mʌtʃ]	viel	15
mushroom ['mʌʃrʊm]	Pilz	15
nice [naɪs]	nett	15
oil [ɔɪl]	Öl	15
pay [peɪ]	zahlen	15
petrol ['petrəl]	Benzin	15
prepare [prɪ'peə]	vorbereiten	15
progress ['prəʊgres]	Fortschritt	15
rescue ['reskjuː]	retten	15
region ['riːdʒən]	Gegend	15
right [raɪt]	richtig	15
river ['rɪvə]	Fluß	15
safety ['seɪfti]	Sicherheit	15
severe shock [sɪ'vɪə ʃɒk]	schlimmer Schock	15
state [steɪt]	Zustand	15
suffer from ['sʌfə frɒm]	leiden an	15
thrilled ['θrɪld]	(freudig) erregt	15
timetable ['taɪmˌteɪbl]	Fahrplan	15
victim ['vɪktɪm]	Opfer	15
village ['vɪlɪdʒ]	Dorf	15
violin [ˌvaɪə'lɪn]	Geige	15
activity [æk'tɪvɪti]	Tätigkeit	16
ahead [ə'hed]	kommend	16
apron ['eɪprən]	Schürze	16
because [bɪ'kɒz]	weil	16
better ['betə]	lieber, besser	16
catch [kætʃ]	fangen	16
championship ['tʃæmpjənʃɪp]	Meisterschaft	16
channel ['tʃænəl]	Kanal	16
civil status ['sɪvɪl'steɪtəs]	(Familien-)Stand	16
coastal ['kəʊstəl]	Küsten-	16
cold [kəʊld]	kalt	16
collect [kə'lekt]	sammeln	16
crash helmet ['kræʃˌhelmɪt]	Sturzhelm	16
dark [dɑːk]	dunkel	16
director [dɪ'rektə]	Regisseur	16
divorce [dɪ'vɔːs]	sich scheiden lassen	16
during ['djʊərɪŋ]	während	16
eagle [iːgl]	Adler	16
eat [iːt]	essen	16
exotic [ɪg'sɒtɪk]	exotisch	16

neues Wort	Übersetzung	unit
expensive [ɪk'spensɪv]	teuer	16
ferry [ferɪ]	Fähre	16
global ['gləʊbl]	Welt-	16
guest [gest]	Gast	16
hard work [ˌhɑːd 'wɜːk]	harte Arbeit	16
hot [hɒt]	heiß	16
including [ɪn'kluːdɪŋ]	eingeschlossen	16
Indian chief ['ɪndjən tʃiːf]	Indianerhäuptling	16
land [lænd]	Land	16
leotard ['liːəʊtɑːd]	Sporttrikot	16
local ['ləʊkl]	örtlich	16
married ['mærɪd]	verheiratet	16
motorbike ['məʊtəbaɪk]	Motorrad	16
nearly ['nɪəlɪ]	fast	16
not any more [nɒt enɪ mɔː]	nicht mehr	16
Phew! [fjuː]	Pfui!	16
plan [plæn]	Plan	16
pyramid ['pɪrəmɪd]	Pyramide	16
queen [kwiːn]	Königin	16
rain [reɪn]	Regen	16
ride [raɪd]	fahren, reiten	16
rough [rʌf]	rauh, ungemütlich	16
round [raʊnd]	rund(herum)	16
same [seɪm]	der-/die-/dasselbe	16
seafood ['siːfuːd]	Meeresfrüchte	16
seasickness pill ['siːsɪknɪs pɪl]	Tablette gegen Seekrankheit	16
shorts [ʃɔːts]	kurze Hose	16
space [speɪs]	Weltall	16
spacesuit ['speɪssuːt]	Raumanzug	16
spend [spend]	verbringen	16
suit [suːt]	Anzug	16
sunbathe ['sʌnbeɪð]	sonnenbaden	16
suntan oil ['sʌntæn ɔɪl]	Sonnenschutzöl	16
swim [swɪm]	schwimmen	16
television guide ['telɪˌvɪʒngaɪd]	Fernsehzeitung	16
through [θruː]	durch	16
together [tə'geðə]	zusammen	16
villainous ['vɪlənəs]	schurkisch	16
visually ['vɪzjʊəlɪ]	visuell	16
walk [wɔːk]	spazierengehen	16
wear [weə]	tragen	16
weather ['weðə]	Wetter	16
win [wɪn]	gewinnen	16
wing [wɪŋ]	Schwinge, Flügel	16
anything ['enɪθɪŋ]	irgend etwas	17
awful ['ɔːfʊl]	schrecklich	17
background ['bækgraʊnd]	Hintergrund	17
ballet ['bæleɪ]	Ballett	17
banker ['bæŋkə]	Bankdirektor	17
bath [bɑːθ]	Bad	17
boring ['bɔːrɪŋ]	langweilig	17
bought [bɔːt]	kaufte	17
child [tʃaɪld]	Kind	17
did [dɪd]	tat, machte	17
drove [drəʊv]	fuhr	17
face [feɪs]	Gesicht	17
fell asleep [ˌfelə'sliːp]	schlief ein	17
grandmother ['grænˌmʌðə]	Großmutter	17
great [greɪt]	prima	17
happen ['hæpən]	geschehen	17
hour ['aʊə]	Stunde	17
I'll write [aɪl 'raɪt]	ich werde schreiben	17
illness ['ɪlnɪs]	Krankheit	17
into ['ɪntʊ]	in (hinein)	17
journal ['dʒɜːnl]	Zeitschrift	17
kill [kɪl]	töten	17
last night [lɑːst'naɪt]	gestern abend	17
medical ['medɪkl]	medizinisch	17
money [mʌnɪ]	Geld	17
nearly ['nɪəlɪ]	fast	17
out [aʊt]	aus (heraus)	17
over ['əʊvə]	(hin-)über	17
position [pə'zɪʃən]	Dienst(rang)	17
push [pʊʃ]	stoßen	17
science fiction film [ˌsaɪəns'fɪkʃn'fɪlm]	Zukunftsfilm	17
scream [skriːm]	schreien	17
shopping ['ʃɒpɪŋ]	Einkaufen	17
show [ʃəʊ]	Vorstellung	17
signed [saɪnd]	unterschrieben	17
since [sɪns]	seit	17

neues Wort	Übersetzung	unit
stop [stɒp]	anhalten	17
story ['stɔːrɪ]	Geschichte	17
sudden ['sʌdən]	plötzlich	17
surprise [sə'praɪz]	Überraschung	17
thought [θɔːt]	dachte	17
threw [θruː]	warf(en)	17
throw [θrəʊ]	werfen	17
towards [tʊ'wɔːds]	in Richtung	17
wheel [wiːl]	Lenkrad	17
whole [həʊl]	ganz	17
act [ækt]	(eine Rolle) spielen	18
actress ['æktrɪs]	Schauspielerin	18
apple ['æpl]	Apfel	18
attack [ə'tæk]	angreifen	18
be lucky [bi: 'lʌkɪ]	Glück haben	18
birth [bɜːθ]	Geburt	18
blind [blaɪnd]	blenden	18
born [bɔːn]	geboren	18
busy ['bɪzi]	beschäftigt	18
climber ['klaɪmə]	Bergsteiger	18
compose [kɒm'pəʊz]	komponieren	18
conqueror ['kɒnkərə]	Eroberer	18
convince [kən'vɪns]	überzeugen	18
design [dɪ'zaɪn]	entwerfen	18
discover [dɪs'kʌvə]	entdecken	18
discoverer [dɪs'kʌvərə]	Entdecker	18
example [ɪg'zɑːmpl]	Beispiel	18
fall [fɔːl]	Sturz	18
guy [gaɪ]	Mann, Kerl	18
headache ['hedeɪk]	Kopfschmerzen	18
helicopter ['helɪkɒptə]	Hubschrauber	18
horse [hɔːs]	Pferd	18
hovercraft ['hɒvəkrɑːft]	Luftkissenfahrzeug	18
invent [ɪn'vent]	erfinden	18
investigation [ɪnˌvestɪ'geɪʃən]	Untersuchung	18
it doesn't matter [ɪt'dʌznt'mætə]	das macht nichts	18
knife [naɪf]	Messer	18
ledge [ledʒ]	Vorsprung	18
meeting ['miːtɪŋ]	Treffen, Versammlung	18
miss [mɪs]	verpassen	18
most [məʊst]	am meisten	18
not to worry [ˌnɒtə'wʌri]	kein Grund zur Sorge	18
novel ['nɒvəl]	Roman	18
on time [ɒn'taɪm]	pünktlich	18
part [pɑːt]	Rolle	18
playwright ['pleɪraɪt]	Stückeschreiber	18
project ['prɒdʒekt]	durchdringen lassen	18
psychiatrist [saɪ'kaɪətrɪst]	Psychiater	18
rescue ['reskjuː]	Rettung	18
return [rɪ'tɜːn]	zurückkehren	18
ring [rɪŋ]	anrufen	18
safe [seɪf]	sicher	18
save [seɪv]	retten	18
survive [sə'vaɪv]	überleben	18
tree [triː]	Baum	18
voice [vɔɪs]	Stimme	18
writer ['raɪtə]	Schriftsteller(in)	18
actually ['æktʃʊəlɪ]	wirklich	19
Africa ['æfrɪkə]	Afrika	19
attractive [ə'træktɪv]	attraktiv	19
before [bɪ'fɔː]	vor	19
boss [bɒs]	Chef	19
butterfly ['bʌtəflaɪ]	Schmetterling	19
come round [kʌm'raʊnd]	vorbeikommen	19
customer ['kʌstəmə]	Kunde	19
false [fɔːls]	falsch	19
finger nail ['fɪŋgəˌneɪl]	Fingernagel	19
grass [grɑːs]	Gras	19
have to ['hævtʊ]	müssen	19
horn [hɔːn]	Horn	19
hunter ['hʌntə]	Jäger	19
I'm afraid [aɪmə'freɪd]	tut mir leid	19
leaf [liːf]	Blatt	19
letter ['letə]	Brief	19
mouth [maʊθ]	Mund	19
office ['ɒfɪs]	Büro	19
pack [pæk]	packen	19
philosophy [fɪ'lɒsəfi]	Philosophie	19
plant [plɑːnt]	Pflanze	19
pointed ['pɔɪntɪd]	spitz	19
polite [pə'laɪt]	höflich	19

94